eSuperbrands

YOUR GUIDE TO SOME OF THE BEST BRANDS ON THE WEB 2006

Argentina Australia Austria Baltic States Bulgaria Brazil Canada
China Croatia Czech Republic Denmark Ecuador Egypt Finland France
Germany Greece Hong Kong Hungary Iceland India Indonesia Ireland
Italy Japan Kuwait Lebanon Malaysia Mexico Morocco The Netherlands
Norway Pakistan Philippines Poland Portugal Romania Russia Saudi Arabia
Serbia Singapore Slovakia Slovenia South Africa South Korea Spain Sri Lanka
Sweden Switzerland Taiwan Thailand Turkey United Arab Emirates United Kingdom
United States of America

www.superbrands.org/uk

BRAND LIAISON DIRECTOR
Simon Muldowney
Claire Pollock
Liz Silvester

MANAGING EDITOR
Angela Cooper

EDITORS
Karen Dugdale
Jennifer Small

JUNIOR ACCOUNT EXECUTIVE
Christy Lyons

DESIGNERS
Chris Harris
Adrian Morris

Other publications from Superbrands in the UK include:
Superbrands Volume VII ISBN: 0-9547510-8-6
Business Superbrands Volume IV ISBN: 0-9547510-6-X
CoolBrands Volume IV ISBN: 0-9550824-1-2
Sport BrandLeaders Volume I ISBN: 0-9547510-4-3

For more information, or to order these books, email:
brands@superbrands.org or call: 01825 723398.

For Superbrands international publications email:
brands@superbrands.org or call 0207 379 8884.

© 2005 Superbrands Ltd

Published by Superbrands Ltd
19 Garrick Street
London
WC2E 9AX

www.superbrands.org/uk

Printed in China

ISBN: 1-905652-00-3

JOHN NOBLE
Director
British Brands Group

The British Brands Group is delighted to support this latest edition of eSuperbrands. On the following pages you will find a diverse range of online brands. Some have evolved exclusively in the online environment while others were established long before the web existed, using the channel to strengthen relationships with their consumer and to meet needs more effectively.

The diversity of the sites depicted illustrates and celebrates the diversity of branding. Each gives the consumer a relevant, distinctive experience while providing real solutions to make lives richer and easier.

Brands in the online world are particularly important. Users seek simple ways to navigate the plethora of offers available and reassurance that they can rely on sites to deliver. The eSuperbrands listed here provide these beacons of familiarity and trust. They also appreciate that, to sustain this relationship with their customers, they must continue to invest, evolve and innovate.

PAUL GOSTICK
International Chairman
The Chartered Institute of Marketing (CIM)

The web collapses the brand promise and sales cycle to seconds. Smart companies use the internet to create a richer brand experience to strengthen customer relationships and their brand promise across all channels. An integrated approach is required, covering everything from the website, to fulfilment of the offer.

Before the dotcom bubble burst, eBranding owed more to a gold-rush mentality than sound marketing and consumer need. Since then, marketing has matured, with online brands representing a significant proportion of the propositions that we encounter on a daily basis. Across all sectors, eBranding is the vehicle that can carry messages globally at the touch of a button.

The Chartered Institute of Marketing is proud to endorse the return of eSuperbrands, which independently identifies many of the UK's most successful and respected online brands. It offers a keen insight into the organisations to determine exactly what sets them apart from the rest.

VALERIE SCHAFER
IPA E-commerce and New Media Consultant
IPA

I was working in digital media in 1994 when the sector was still in its infancy. Around that time, I remember watching a Nissan TV ad that ended its spot with www.nissan.com. It was at this very moment that I knew 'online' was about to explode and that the internet was going to transform communication going forward – in every way.

Over the past decade the stunning growth of the sector has not abated. It continues to leap past other media in terms of popularity and effectiveness. That's because its essence is truly global, genuinely democratic and uniquely interactive...and it's only just beginning!

Where the medium goes from here is anybody's guess. But one thing is sure – digital is here to stay and will continue to thrive at a fever pitch for many years to come. This book salutes those businesses embracing the e-brand phenomenon and the IPA wholeheartedly does too.

About eSuperbrands

This publication forms part of a pioneering and exciting programme that was founded with the aim of paying tribute to the UK's strongest ebrands.

A dedicated eSuperbrands council (listed below) has been formulated, consisting of eminent individuals who are well qualified to judge which are the nation's strongest ebrands. Each brand featured in this book has been given eSuperbrand status based on the ranking of this council.

Through identifying these brands, and providing their case histories, the organisation hopes that people will gain a greater appreciation of the discipline of branding and a greater admiration for the brands themselves.

eSuperbrands Council 2006

Wayne Arnold
Managing Director
Profero

David Day
Managing Director
– EMEA Region
Nielsen//NetRatings

Brent Hoberman
Co-founder
lastminute.com

Jody Haskayne
Director of PR
& Communications
Tiscali UK Limited

Rachel Johnson
VP Marketing Europe
Ask Jeeves Inc.

Lisa Jones
Editor
.net

Michael Murphy
Chief Executive Officer
Friends Reunited

John Owen
Chairman
IPA's Digital Marketing Group

Steve Perry
Marketing Services Director
NTL

Donna Price
Chairperson
eSuperbrands Council

Timothy Ryan
Brand Marketing Director
AOL UK

James Sanderson
Joint Managing Director
glue London

Rory Sutherland
Vice-Chairman
The Ogilvy Group, UK

Simon Waldman
Director of Digital Publishing
Guardian

Contents

Foreword

Angela Cooper
Managing Editor

How could we cope without the internet? A question that the millions of us, from all corners of the world, who use the internet on a daily basis often muse over. It is quite incredible to think that 10 years ago few of us would have used the internet, or indeed believed that we would come to rely upon it as a vital resource which transcends our daily lives.

With its roots in the packet-switching networks of the 1960s, it was the realisation of how the technology could be used which marked a significant breakthrough. In 1991, Tim Berners-Lee invented a standard linked information system, which could be accessed by all the various types of computers that were in use at the time. This became what we now refer to as the World Wide Web. Over the next 10 years, widespread use of the web grew, then snowballed – igniting the entrepreneurial spirit in many. This ensued a crash of equally phenomenal proportions, leaving only the fittest still standing.

Now, in the relative calm after the storm, you will find in the pages that follow, case studies of the brands which have emerged from the fight as some of the strongest players in the field. These brands are particularly admirable as they have come such a long way in their short lifetimes, beating off fierce global competition and seen so many of their peers fall.

The eSuperbrands book is published by the Superbrands organisation – the independent authority on branding. The organisation promotes the discipline of branding and pays tribute to exceptional brands.

The independent and voluntary eSuperbrands Council (see page 12) have rated the brands that appear in eSuperbrands as being some of the strongest in the market.

" The power of the web is in its universality. Access by everyone regardless of disability is an essential aspect. "

Tim Berners-Lee Inventor of the World Wide Web

" Basically, our goal is to organize the world's information and to make it universally accessible and useful. "

Larry Page
Co-founder of Google

" Sometimes we get taken by surprise. For example when the internet came along, we had it as 5th or 6th priority. "

Bill Gates, speaking in 1998

" Advances in computer technology and the internet have changed the way America works, learns, and communicates. The internet has become an integral part of America's economic, political, and social life. "

Bill Clinton President of the United States 1993 – 2001

" The internet is based on a layered, end-to-end model that allows people at each level of the network to innovate free of any central control. By placing intelligence at the edges rather than control in the middle of the network, the internet has created a platform for innovation. "

Vinton Cerf
American computer scientist, commonly referred to as 'father of the internet'.

" The internet revolution is going to be like all the other revolutions we have seen in history. It's going to be over before a lot of us even know it started. "

Adolfo Suarez
Spanish Prime minister 1976 –1981

" The value of information about information can be greater than the value of the information itself. "

Nicholas Negroponte
Founding Chairman of MIT's Media Laboratory and author of best-seller 'Being Digital'.

" The internet is the Viagra of big business. "
Jack Welch Former General Electric Chairman and CEO

" It may not always be profitable at first for businesses to be online, but it is certainly going to be unprofitable not to be online. "

Esther Dyson Noted consultant and philosopher in the field of digital technology.

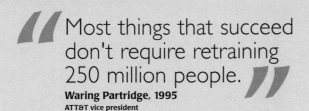

Most things that succeed don't require retraining 250 million people.

Waring Partridge, 1995
ATT&T vice president

I agree completely with my son James when he says 'the internet is like electricity. The latter lights up everything, while the former lights up knowledge'.

Kerry Packer
Australian publishing, media and gaming tycoon

I used to think that cyberspace was 50 years away. What I thought was 50 years away, was only 10 years away. And what I thought was 10 years away... it was already here. I just wasn't aware of it yet.

Bruce Sterling   Science fiction writer and internationally recognised as a cyberspace theorist.

The internet is becoming the town square for the global village of tomorrow.

Bill Gates   Co-founder and Chief Software Architect of Microsoft Corporation and the world's richest man.

When I took office, only high energy physicists had ever heard of what is called the World Wide Web. Now even my cat has its own page.

Bill Clinton
President of the United States 1993 – 2001

I predict the Internet will soon go spectacularly supernova and in 1996 catastrophically collapse.

Robert Metcalfe, 1995
Author, 3Com founder and Ethernet developer

We techies should be more honest about what computers can do and what they cannot do, or else we are setting ourselves up for a big pie in the face.

Clifford Stoll, 1995
Astronomer, author and computer systems administrator

They say a marketer's and consumer's dream is the World Wide Web. It's the best of mass advertising and the best of target marketing.

David King of DDB Needham

Any sufficiently advanced technology is indistinguishable from magic.

Arthur C. Clarke
Inventor and Science Fiction author

eSuperbrands Council

01 Wayne Arnold
Managing Director
Profero
www.profero.com

02 David Day
Managing Director
– EMEA Region
Nielsen//NetRatings
www.nielsen-netratings.com

03 Brent Hoberman
Co-founder
lastminute.com
www.lastminute.com

04 Jody Haskayne
Director of PR
& Communications
Tiscali UK Limited
www.tiscali.co.uk

05 Rachel Johnson
VP Marketing Europe
Ask Jeeves Inc.
www.ask.co.uk

06 Lisa Jones
Editor
.net
www.netmag.co.uk

07 Michael Murphy
Chief Executive Officer
Friends Reunited
www.friendsreunited.co.uk

09 Steve Perry
Marketing Services Director
NTL
www.ntl.com

11 Timothy Ryan
Brand Marketing Director
AOL UK
www.aol.com

08 John Owen
Chairman
IPA's Digital Marketing Group
www.ipa.co.uk

10 Donna Price
Chairperson
eSuperbrands Council
www.superbrands.org/uk

12 James Sanderson
Joint Managing Director
glue London
www.gluelondon.com

13 Rory Sutherland
Vice-Chairman,
The Ogilvy Group, UK
www.ogilvy.com

14 Simon Waldman
Director of Digital Publishing
Guardian
www.guardian.co.uk

01 Wayne Arnold
Managing Director
Profero
www.profero.com

Wayne is one of the digital industry's most experienced practitioners, and together with his brother Daryl, he co-founded Profero in 1998.

Profero has grown to become Europe and Asia's largest digital independent and Wayne as MD has successfully supervised campaigns for an enviable client list including Apple, Ask Jeeves, AstraZeneca, Black and Decker, Channel 4, Central Office of Information, Disney BVI and Merrill Lynch Investment Managers.

Profero currently have offices in Australia, China, France, Germany, Hong Kong, Italy, Japan, Spain, Singapore and the UK.

Wayne currently acts as the Vice Chairman of the Institute of Practitioners in Advertising's (IPA) Digital Marketing Group and sits on the council.

05 Rachel Johnson
VP Marketing Europe
Ask Jeeves Inc.
www.ask.co.uk

Rachel is responsible for the strategic development of the European Marketing Plan, supporting the global brand strategy for Ask Jeeves in the UK and Europe. She is accountable for managing the implementation of all TTL activity and is a member of the European Executive Committee for Ask Jeeves.

Rachel joined Ask Jeeves from Levi Strauss & Co where she held the role of Marketing Director Northern Europe. Previous roles held during her time at the company include Acting UK Country Managing Director and Marketing Manager North Europe.

Rachel's extensive marketing experience has also included roles for Whitbread Beer Co. as Marketing Manager for the Heineken brand where she drove the strategic re-positioning of the brand in the UK and with SmithKline Beecham as a Group Product Manager.

02 David Day
Managing Director – EMEA Region
Nielsen//NetRatings
www.nielsen-netratings.com

As Managing Director for Europe, the Middle East and Africa, David is responsible for managing all aspects of the commercial and operational sides of the business.

With a background in research and statistics, David joined ACNielsen in 1997 as Head of Statistical Services and became Director of Operations for the UK in 1998. He joined Nielsen//NetRatings in 2000 as Director of Analytics – International. In 2002, David became Senior Vice President, Commercial in the International Division. In this role, David was instrumental in growing the business in the company's key markets outside the US.

Educated at University College London, David holds a BA Hons and Ph.D in Physics. He spent a number of years with the UK Government Statistical Service. While there he was trained in statistics at the University of Greenwich and was later awarded an MBA by Imperial College where he specialised in the New Economy.

06 Lisa Jones
Editor
.net
www.netmag.co.uk

Lisa is the editor of .net, the UK's best selling monthly internet magazine (www.netmag.co.uk). Established in 1995, .net is the definitive guide to the web for advanced users and professionals.

Previously editor of Internet Works and contributor to a variety of technology titles, Lisa has also worked in online marketing, and regularly provides expert comment on internet and technology issues for television, radio and newspapers. Lisa has a BA degree in English, an MA in Cultural Politics from Cardiff University and a certificate from the Chartered Institute of Marketing.

03 Brent Hoberman
Co-founder
lastminute.com
www.lastminute.com

Brent co-founded lastminute.com in April 1998, with Martha Lane Fox, in the living room of his London flat three years after having drafted the initial idea. Brent was 29 and Martha was just 25.

lastminute.com offers consumers airline tickets, car hire, hotel rooms, package holidays, entertainment tickets, restaurant reservations, home delivery, speciality services, gifts and auctions. Brent's initial vision remains unchanged – 'to delight customers with great value, inspiration and solutions when they are going away, going out or staying in.'

The company floated in March 2000 when the dotcom bubble was at its peak. Seven years on the company is the number one travel website in Europe and was acquired by Travelocity Europe for $1.1 billion, a division of Sabre Holdings Corporation on 20th July 2005.

Brent's entrepreneurial vision ensures the lastminute.com customer experience is continually enhanced by the latest innovations in technology.

Brent, now 36, was born in South Africa, educated at Eton and holds a MA in French and German literature from Oxford. He lives in central London with his wife, Genevieve and two daughters.

04 Jody Haskayne
Director of PR & Communications
Tiscali UK Limited
www.tiscali.co.uk

Jody joined Tiscali in February 2003 to head all PR & Communications activity, including Corporate, Consumer, Business and Public Affairs programmes.

With seven years' experience in Technology and Consumer PR she worked previously as Account Director in various PR agencies across many brands on UK, Pan European and Global PR campaigns.

Prior to PR specialisation, she worked in broader marcoms, software partnerships and sales roles for the Moore Corporation, a global print and logistics company.

As a Physics Graduate Jody began her career as a mathematics teacher in Liverpool.

07 Michael Murphy
Chief Executive Officer
Friends Reunited
www.friendsreunited.co.uk

Michael, 40, was appointed Chief Executive Officer of Friends Reunited in February 2003. Prior to this appointment, Michael had a 20 year career with Pearson plc, culminating in being Chief Operating Officer of the Financial Times. He left the Financial Times in April 2002 to pursue a management buy out of one of its divisions. When this failed to materialise in July 2002, Michael continued to work with a number of venture capitalists to find a management buy-in opportunity. It was in January 2003 that he finally achieved his aim of an MBI although this was eventually completed without any bank or venture capitalist involvement.

Before taking the position of Chief Operating Officer at the Financial Times he held the same position at FT.com where he helped the site break even and introduced subscription charges. He was also Managing Director of Financial Times Business where he re-focused the company as a specialist publisher of market leading magazines.

08 John Owen
Chairman
IPA's Digital Marketing Group
www.ipa.co.uk

John is the planning partner of leading digital marketing agency, Dare, and chairman of the IPA's Digital Marketing Group.

Dare, which counts the AA, Barclays Group, COI, Sony Ericsson, Travelocity, Unilever, Wanadoo and Woolworths among its key clients, has won Campaign 'Digital Agency of the Year' for the past two years and is also Revolution's 'Agency of the Year'.

John's earlier career was in journalism, latterly as the news editor of Campaign. He moved to the media communications agency, Motive, in 1999, where he set up the digital unit. A year later, following Motive's merger with Starcom, he became director of Starcom IP, which grew into a top 10 online media agency during his tenure, representing clients such as Barclays, Levi's and One 2 One.

He joined Dare in August 2003 and has put the discipline of account planning at the heart of the agency's approach to digital marketing.

09 Steve Perry
Marketing Services Director
NTL
www.ntl.com

Steve has been at NTL since April 2000. As Marketing Services Director, his primary focus is the strategic and operational management of NTL's 'owned' and third party marketing inventory, as well as the development and launch of new, 'non-traditional' channels to market.

During his time at NTL, he has been responsible for content production of the customer ISP portal, ntlworld.com and Interactive TV 'walled-garden' site, as well as all online sales and marketing via the ntl.com website.

His team has also launched and managed a number of acquisition and customer service TV channels across the NTL and Sky platforms.

Prior to NTL, Steve spent 10 years as a new-media consultant for companies such as Sky, S4C and Cable & Wireless.

12 James Sanderson
Joint Managing Director
glue London
www.gluelondon.com

James has worked in digital communications since 1999 having spent the previous decade working in advertising agencies as well as for the advertising bible Campaign.

In 2002 he joined glue London, an advertising agency specialising in digital, having finally worked out that 'digital' and 'advertising' were two worlds that were about to collide with extraordinary consequences.

Since then glue has become one of the fastest growing agencies in the UK, growing from 20 to over 80 staff. The agency has won dozens of creative awards, is consistently voted as the most respected in the business and was voted the 'Best of the Best' by the IPA in 2005.

Through glue James spends his time working with some of the largest advertisers in Europe including Eurostar, Masterfoods, McDonald's, P&G and Virgin helping them embrace the vast opportunity that digital has to offer.

10 Donna Price
Chairperson
eSuperbrands Council
www.superbrands.org/uk

Donna joined Superbrands as Commercial Director in April 2005 at the start of the eSuperbrands Council process. In her role as Commercial Director she heads up the UK operation and is responsible for the marketing, PR, editorial and sales process for all of the UK programmes. She also chairs three other Superbrands Council's including, Kids Superbrands, Superbrands and CoolBrands. Previously, Donna spent three years at The Mirror Group where she was responsible for the launch of both M magazine and M Celebs. Both of these launches represented a significant strategic move to take The Mirror slightly more upmarket. Prior to this she worked at Emap for nine years where she worked on some of the UK's premiere magazine brands including Elle, FHM, Sky, Mixmag and Kerrang! Her experience spans a mixture of advertising, marketing and publishing.

13 Rory Sutherland
Vice-Chairman
The Ogilvy Group, UK
www.ogilvy.com

Rory joined OgilvyOne as a graduate trainee in 1988. After a spell as the world's worst account man, he was moved first to the Planning Department and then, more successfully, to the creative department, where he learnt his trade as a copywriter. It was his brief spell in Planning however that first introduced him to online information systems accessible over a squeaky thing called a modem, then operating at a 'blistering' 14.4Kbps, sparking off an undying interest in all things online.

As a copywriter, Rory was promoted to Head of Copy in 1995 and Creative Director in 1997. He is now Executive Creative Director at OgilvyOne Worldwide and Vice Chairman of The Ogilvy Group in the UK. He is married with twin daughters, Hetty and Millie, and lives in Brasted in Kent.

11 Timothy Ryan
Brand Marketing Director
AOL UK
www.aol.com

Timothy has spent the past 15 years working in and around technology and telecoms brands and their marketing. Starting in a marketing consultancy in San Francisco during the early 1990s software boom, then lured by the siren's call of advertising and the bright lights of London, he moved to Saatchi & Saatchi as an account planner, via FutureBrand as European Director of the Telecoms and Technology practice. He then moved to the bright side of life as a client at Orange as Head of Brand Strategy. Now at AOL as Brand Marketing Director, he is continually fascinated by the cross-over of technology and brands and their power to change the way that consumers, companies and governments live, love, lie and laugh. Life beyond technology brands is taken up with fine wine, all things Italian, colourful trousers and things that go bang…!

14 Simon Waldman
Director of Digital Publishing
Guardian
www.guardian.co.uk

Simon joined Guardian newspapers in 1996 to work on some of the company's earliest forays onto the internet.

He was launch editor of Guardian Unlimited in 1999 before moving into general management and becoming the company's first director of digital publishing in 2001. Guardian Unlimited has been named the best daily newspaper on the net for the last five years in the UK newspaper awards, and recently won the newspaper category in the international Webby Awards, ahead of the New York Times and Washington Post.

Simon received the Chairman's award at the 2004 Association of Online Publishers' Awards ceremony for his contribution to the industry.

Before joining Guardian Unlimited Simon was a freelance journalist specialising in media and technology. His first job, however, was a long way from this: as trainee reporter on Shoe and Leather News.

He is married with a daughter.

Market Context

Searching online is now one of the easiest and most popular ways to find a new job. But with more than 500 job boards in the UK and Ireland, as well as thousands of recruitment agencies and employer websites, searching them all has become impossible.

1Job.co.uk provides a centralised search engine for finding jobs on the internet. By using unique vertical search engine technology, 1Job.co.uk delivers job hunters directly to more than 120,000 fresh job adverts from hundreds of websites across the UK and Ireland.

Current advertisers on 1Job.co.uk include job boards, recruitment agencies and employers running recruitment-based marketing campaigns, where quality and quantity of potential vacancy candidates is important.

1Job.co.uk has become a favourite bookmarked site with all types of job hunters and has grown rapidly since its launch in 2004.

Achievements

The 1Job.co.uk brand is now recognised as providing instant access to jobs in all industry sectors in all locations of the UK and Ireland. In May 2005, 1Job.co.uk had more than 120,000 jobs in its index, all of which were less than five days old and received more than 50 million advert views.

By providing a quick and easy centralised place to job search, 1Job.co.uk is able to drive an extremely high number of targeted leads to its customers' job vacancies and websites.

1Job.co.uk has been one of the first websites to fully embrace the concept and benefits of XML and its power when combined with their vertical search engine. This technology is used to enable the job listings and search results to be viewed in different ways, using RSS Readers, WebTV, interactive TV, mobile phones and other handheld devices.

Products and Services

Visitors to 1Job.co.uk can sign up for email alerts of new vacancy opportunities that fit their specified requirements. They can search using keywords to find jobs, or browse the fully categorised job directories.

Job boards and larger recruitment agencies utilise the 1Job.co.uk unique Pay Per Click (PPC) service to advertise hundreds or even thousands of jobs automatically. Unlike traditional search engine PPC advertising, 1Job's system generates and displays current job detail summaries extracted from the full adverts on the recruiter's website.

HISTORY

2002 – Online recruitment market and vertical search engine technology research work commences.

2003 – Vertical search engine prototypes 'Ted', 'Sid' and 'Col' are built.

2003 – 1Job.co.uk beta search engine launches with more than 30,000 jobs in the index.

2004 – More than 70,000 jobs are listed. Visitor numbers increase rapidly as the 1Job.co.uk site becomes heavily bookmarked.

All the original job description text is used and resolved for maximum keyword searching effectiveness. With 1Job.co.uk, each job on a client's website also now becomes an advert for their site.

1Job.co.uk caters successfully for all types of advertiser requirements, from the simplest text and banner adverts right through to ad agency-designed recruitment campaigns that can utilise 1Job.co.uk's fully hosted MicroSites™.

Career- and training-related adverts are also catered for. Active-hyperlink text or image adverts can be uploaded onto the site easily in banner- or side-advert format. Custom-built adverts and campaigns are also provided and welcomed.

THINGS YOU DIDN'T KNOW...

The site is privately funded and was designed and built by two people – Julian Felstead and Kerry Torchia.

The hi-tech and sophisticated indexing software that visits thousands of pages each day has been named after a 'Fast Show' character and is now affectionately known as Colin.

The trial of 1Job, with 70,000 adverts and thousands of visitor searches, was undertaken on a £29 per month server. This was to test the robustness of the software.

Personality and Goals

Characterised by the smiley faces in the search results when a direct link to an advert is available, or by the 'Cartoon of the Day' slot, 1Job.co.uk tries to maintain the same friendly, approachable relationship with all customers, visitors and suppliers.

The company's vision is to establish itself as the primary starting point for any job seeker's search. To this end, 1Job.co.uk is always focused on improving content and ease of finding that content. For advertisers, the company focus is on sourcing quality candidates to any type of advert displayed, with advert delivery from the website, by email, interactive TV or mobile devices.

www.1job.co.uk

2004 – Beta testing and development continues with extra services such as job posting, job alerts, saved searches successfully rolled out.

2004 – 1JobIreland.com launched specifically for job hunters in Ireland.

2005 – 1Job is recognised in Onrec's 'Top 100 Online Recruitment Sites' guide listed at number three for jobs in 2004. More than 100,000 jobs listed daily.

2005 – Partnerships with major job boards, portals and other companies formed.

2005 – XML feeds added enabling site users to directly use and receive search results onto their own PC desktop readers and other devices.

Market Context

Since its launch in 2000, 192.com has become more than just a directory enquiry service. It is now a fully operational people and business finder site that offers over 160 million records.

The business information market is worth over £1 billion a year in the UK and some of the key players include, Thomson Directories, Yell.com, Dun and Bradstreet (DnB) and British Telecom (BT).

Unlike many of its competitors 192.com resisted the temptation to raise and spend large sums of capital during the dotcom boom and bust period, choosing instead to rely on its flourishing 'word-of-mouth' reputation. This enabled 192.com to expand organically and achieve considerable market success with no significant capital outlay.

the first site to license its complete database. This was quickly followed by a full site launch in 2000 that confirmed 192.com as the first comprehensive online directory enquiry site in the UK.

Just a year after its launch 192.com was voted one of the top 100 sites that 'changed the web forever' by .net magazine. Further accolades came in 2004 when 192.com won the 'best online directory site' at the 118 Tracker Awards – beating off competition from Yell.com, BT and Thomson Directories – and in 2005 the same award was bestowed upon 192.com for the second consecutive year.

The site now has over 4.8 million registered users and 3.2 million non-registered users, together contributing to 30 million page impressions a month.

While de-regulation of Directory Enquiries promised more enhanced directory services, few businesses have sourced the data sets to deliver these services as effectively as 192.com.

192.com currently has over 25% of the online directory enquiry market (Source: Nielsen Ratings) and handles over 80 million searches a year.

Products and Services

192.com licenses the most comprehensive residential and business data sets, combining them to create a fully enhanced database. This includes the full range of data that a traditional directory service has – free of charge – but also includes value-added data, for instance, maps, route plotters, aerial photos and property prices.

192.com publishes residential data that includes, Electoral Roll data from 2002-2005 and a directory enquiry database with 13 million residential telephone listings. One of its unique services is enhanced residential and business data at cost-effective prices; users can purchase

Achievements

It was in 1999 that 192.com's parent company i-CD took the pioneering step towards full de-regulation of Directory Enquiries, when it became

HISTORY

1999 – 192.com's parent company i-CD becomes the first licensee of BT's directory enquiry database and goes on to licence the entire DnB business data set.

2000 – 192.com launches as the first directory enquiry site in the UK. It offers listings, information from the Electoral Roll and DnB business data.

2002 – 192.com's user base reaches two million.

2002 – 192.com voted one of the 100 sites to 'change the internet forever' by .net magazine.

'credit packages' enabling them to search the Electoral Roll and view company and director reports.

192.com has developed powerful search facilities for the Electoral Roll data that enables consumers to search by name only or by relationship. For example, it allows a search for every John Smith that lives with a Mary Reynolds.

As well as detailed residential information 192.com publishes business data from a variety of sources: Directory Enquiries, Classified Business Listings from Thomson, DnB's UK Marketing File and The Director and Shareholder Database, that includes snapshots of financial data on over two million companies and information on 3.4 million individual directors.

SERIOUSLY, YOU CAN **FIND ANYONE**

1 9ʷˣʸᶻ 2ᵃᵇᶜ .com
People, Places & Business

Enter person | Search Now

Personality and Goals

192.com offers an innovative and comprehensive service in the provision of directory services. Within the information provision remit 192.com's personality is 'David' to the industry's 'Goliath': entrepreneurial, young and ambitious. Its brand values remain responsive, informed and pioneering, setting a high standard in the competitive directory service market with its ever-changing demands.

www.192.com

2003 – 192.com's user-base increases to 3.5 million.

2003 – De-regulation of Directory Enquiries sees a massive drop-off in calls to voice services – which stood at about 35% of the market-share before de-regulation.

2005 – Since de-regulation, 192.com's user base reaches 4.8 million and traffic increases by 400%.

2005 – 192.com launches the first of three new look sites with the aim of becoming the definitive local search engine for both people and businesses.

2005 – The 192.com database reaches 160 million records.

Market Context

There were almost 20 million over-50s in the UK in 2000. By 2025 there are expected to be nearly 27 million. This age group currently buys 80% of all top-range cars, 50% of skincare products and 80% of leisure cruises sold in the UK (Source: Senioragency International). In 2002, one fifth of the UK's online population was aged over 50. By 2005 that figure had jumped to a quarter, making the over-50s the fastest-growing audience on the internet, with approximately 6.25 million online (Source: Nielsen//NetRatings). Online spending among the over-55s grew by 129% in 2003, contributing £747 million to the total online market value of £4.9 billion (Source: e-Retail Verdict).

Achievements

50Connect primarily targets 'Baby Boomers' – those aged 45-60. While younger audiences are generally thought to pick up computer skills quickly, most mature users have learnt skills in a white-collar workplace and a high proportion fall into the ABC1 category, making them discerning online consumers.

Averaging one million unique visitors a month and 130,000 members, 50Connect is by far the largest website for the over-45s in the UK. Its nearest online competitor, Saga.co.uk, has half the number of monthly visitors.

Products and Services

50Connect provides online consumers with the opportunity to live life to the full. The site covers everything from personal finance to relationship advice for the over-45s, producing more than 40 articles in-house each week. 50Connect is a gateway to the wider online world for mature web users, providing informative content, competitions, community, special offers and reviewed links.

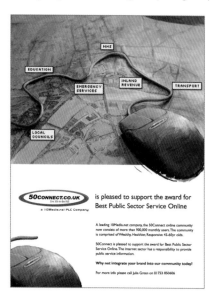

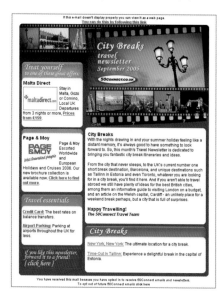

HISTORY

1999 – 50Connect founder Philip Cooper begins proposals for seeking funding for a venture targeting the over-50s market online.

August 2000 – 50Connect.co.uk launches in the UK.

November 2000 – 50Connect trademarks the slogan 'Live Life to The Full'.

March 2001 – 50Connect launches a string of new popular content channels, further strengthening the brand's appeal to the over-45s market.

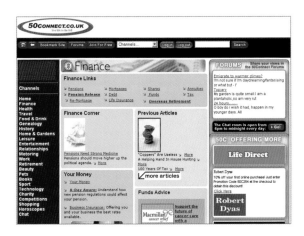

holidays and how to download MP3 music files – highlight the brand's appeal to the young-at-heart 'Baby Boomer'.

Personality and Goals

50Connect is a fun, informative and community-led brand. It aims to fill the gap between youth-conscious under-35 media and more senior-focused publications targeting the 65+ population. 'Baby Boomers' are image conscious, inquisitive and interested in new things. As a brand, 50Connect provides all these things.

www.50connect.co.uk

Unlike many of its competitors, 50Connect makes little reference to being a website specifically for the over-45s. The brand, like the majority of its audience of 'Baby Boomers', is geared towards keeping and acting young. 50Connect avoids taking a condescending tone with its visitors about what they can and cannot do as they get older. Instead, recent features – including topics such as sex tips, adventure

THINGS YOU DIDN'T KNOW...

50Connect is based in Windsor, just a stone's throw from the entrance to the Castle in a building which was once lived in by King Charles II's mistress, Nell Gwynn.

In an online poll, 50Connect members voted former Beatle, Sir Paul McCartney unanimously as their choice for celebrity President of Europe. Tony Blair came last, behind Mo Mowlam and Alan Titchmarsh.

On average there are 1,000 people on the 50Connect.co.uk site at any one time.

2001 – 50Connect.co.uk achieves 50,000 registered members.

2002 – High-profile online advertising and marketing campaigns, signal the site's arrival as the major online brand for the mature market.

2003 – 50Connect membership passes 80,000, while visitor numbers to the site exceed those of Saga.co.uk for the first time.

2004 – 50Connect launches two newsletters – '50Connect Travel' and '50Connect Money' – securing an additional 30,000 members in the process.

2005 – 50Connect.co.uk's Money Channel featured as The Times 'Website of the Week'.

Market Context

The online gaming industry has seen phenomenal growth in the past few years. It is currently riding the wave of internet penetration globally and making gaming more convenient and accessible to a wider audience than ever before.

The global online gaming market is estimated to be worth between US$7-10 billion in 2004 having started from zero in 1995. This represents 3.9% of the total global estimated gaming market, including land-based gaming (Source: Global Betting and Gaming Consultants). GBGC estimates that US gamblers account for 45% of the global online gaming market compared with 31% derived from Europe.

In terms of English language facilities, there are currently 1,193 online casinos, 271 online poker sites, 606 online sports books and 149 online bingo rooms (Source: Casino City). With more than 20 million active member accounts, the largest and most successful online casino and poker website in the world is 888.com (Source: Casino City). Its products include Casino-on-net, Pacific Poker and Betmate.

888.com gained first-mover advantage by setting up offices in the UK in 2001. It has kept its position as the dominant force in the online leisure industry by providing an entertainment experience that is second to none. All of 888.com's software is developed in-house, which allows it to be flexible and adapt to changing market conditions in the 151 countries where it operates. This also ensures maximum security for its users.

Achievements

888.com is the number one gaming site worldwide, (Source: iGamingBusiness Q4 2005) and is the number one global online casino (Source: Comscore).

A leader in online gaming since 1997, 888.com is constantly recognised for its commitment to an uncompromising gaming experience. 888.com is one of the few online gaming companies to be awarded the eCOGRA Seal of Approval for player protection, fair gaming and responsible conduct.

888.com has recently been voted 'Best Online Casino 2005' by readers

HISTORY

1996 – The 888.com group was established.

1997 – 888 Holdings acquires a Gaming License from the Antigua Government and launches its first product Casino-on-Net.com.

2002 – The 888.com umbrella brand launches and introduces two new sub-brands: Pacific Poker, the 888.com online Poker Room, and Reef Club Casino.

2003 – 888.com operations migrate from Antigua to Gibraltar. The Group now operates under the Gibraltar Government Gaming License.

888.com can be played in 11 different languages in 151 countries worldwide. Its support team services every language 24/7.

777.com is owned by 888.com and re-directs back to the 888.com site.

The name 888.com was conceived for several reasons. As well as being unique and memorable, it is also because 888 is a symbol of wealth, luck and prosperity in Asia. The number eight in Cantonese reads as 'Fa', which translated means 'a great fortune in the near future'.

Personality and Goals

With 20 million users, 888.com is the global market leader and as such is perceived in a positive way by its consumers. Its goal is to provide quality entertainment to people who enjoy gaming, by giving them the opportunity to do so in a safe, fun, fair, regulated and secure environment.

www.888.com

of Inside Edge magazine, the UK's first gambling magazine. The Inside Edge Award was voted for by more than 50,000 readers and is the first of its kind in the online gaming industry.

In 2005, 888.com was also the proud recipient of the title of 'Best Online Casino', which was bestowed upon it by the readers of another magazine E-Gaming Review.

Products and Services

888.com has always strived to be at the forefront of internet gaming technology. As well as constantly redefining its current software and products, it is always on the lookout for new technologies and potential games that can be brought to market.

At present 888.com is developing its mobile phone-gaming for both casino and poker. In addition, it is constantly developing new product platforms to add to its offering.

June 2004 – 888.com is granted the eCOGRA Seal of Approval for player protection, fair gaming and responsible conduct.

July 2004 – 888.com becomes the main sponsor of the Premier League side Middlesborough Football Club.

October 2004 – 888.com launches another product, Betmate.com, the Group's Sports Betting Exchange product.

2005 – 888.com now employs more than 750 people and has 20 million users in 151 countries.

September 2005 – 888.com becomes a public company and floats on the London Stock Exchange.

all™cures.com

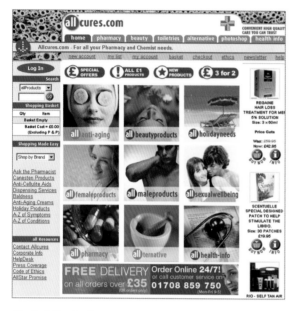

Market Context

In our modern, healthy and image-conscience society, the need for health and beauty products has grown considerably. Buying these products online has evolved into a major new market, helped by new guidelines for companies trading health and pharmaceutical products on the internet. allcures.com, which launched in 1999, has helped considerably in building confidence in this sector.

Nowadays, allcures.com is one of the leading names in health and beauty on the internet, with an enviable reputation for service, quality and excellent advice all at the touch of a button.

Achievements

Before the launch of regulated websites such as allcures.com, health and beauty shopping on the internet could often be a difficult and

uncertain process. The need for guidelines and monitoring were necessary to create an environment in which customers felt confident to buy. allcures.com could see the need for this, and set about developing the website with guidance from the Royal Pharmaceutical Society.

Launched by Jai Cheema in 1999, allcures.com came to market at a risky time for dotcom start-ups. However, the strength of the allcures.com proposition was borne out by it weathering the storm and becoming one of the internet's true survivors.

The company also marked itself out by expanding into a number of services and new product lines. The founders of allcures.com wanted to provide all the services of a local pharmacy but with much more besides. Health advice, prescription dispensing, pharmacists available for advice 24/7 as well as innovative new brands and product availability were all part of its innovative offering, helping allcures.com cement a reputation as much more than just an online store.

Products and Services

allcures.com has products across a vast range of categories, including female and male health and beauty, children's healthcare, sexual health and well-being, alternative medicines as well as everyday essentials. With a range far beyond what the high street has to offer, it aims to be a one-stop-shop for meeting the health and beauty needs of modern Britain.

The anti-ageing boom means that allcures.com has experienced a rapid growth in demand for products such as high-end skincare creams and moisturizers, slimming and skin toning products. As an alternative to expensive and often unnecessary surgery, these products are providing people with an alternative to going under the knife, a choice allcures.com is keen to promote.

Alternative therapy and medicine is another growing area. allcures.com now has a section solely dedicated to its wide range of alternative products, offering herbal remedies, floral remedies, holistic therapy, vitamins and mineral supplements. The scope for the use of these products is becoming as vast as the traditional medicines they aim to replace.

Another boom area is male well-being products. Modern men are expected to moisturise, exfoliate and groom just as much as women. Men now account for over half of the customers who buy from

HISTORY

1999
– allcures.com launches.

2001
– allcures brand is extended to re-branded allcures stores.

2002
– Mike Ritson is appointed as managing director of allcures and heads new online strategies for allcures.com.

allcures.com, with hair loss, skincare and sexual well-being becoming the main draw for male customers on the site.

allcures.com aims to provide the same services one would expect from a high street pharmacy. This includes access to the professional advice of a trained pharmacist, except at allcures.com this service is available 24/7. It also has a dedicated health advice section which highlights conditions, symptoms and remedies. It also plays a proactive role in delivering healthcare messages to people, undertaking health campaigns such as 'Stress in the Workplace' in Canary Wharf and 'Stop Smoking Carbon Monoxide' in Liverpool Street station in London.

THINGS YOU DIDN'T KNOW...

allcures.com sells over 5,000 health and beauty products online, treating everything from acne to high cholesterol.

'Thrush' is the most popular keyword used to search the allcures.com health advice database, closely followed by 'Haemorrhoids' and 'Hair Loss'.

Baldness treatments are the number one seller at allcures.com, accounting for a large proportion of its sales online.

Due to changes in health and beauty trends, men now spend more on products at allcures.com than women. They now account for nearly 60% of allcures.com customers compared to 35% when the site launched in 1999.

allcures.com sets itself apart from the competition with services such as providing NHS dispensing online with free delivery. This is invaluable for those who may be too busy, immobile or live in remote areas of the country.

Personality and Goals

allcures.com is the innovative way to see to all your health, beauty and well-being needs without a trip to the high street pharmacy. The allcures.com style is smart, young and sexy, but also provides the brains and professionalism associated with a visit to the pharmacy. allcures.com's future goals include expanding its diverse product range for the increasing needs of the UK's health-conscious public and further developing the services it can provide online.

www.allcures.com

2003
– allcures move to new premises in South Ockendon, which houses the entire allcures warehouse, head office, IT department and marketing department. In addition, the website is redesigned and re-launched.

2003
– allcures.com launches a number of health campaigns in the UK, including 'Stress in the Workplace', 'Stop Smoking' and 'Holiday Health'.

2005
– allcures.com is named in 'The 50 Best Online Shops' by The Independent newspaper.

Market Context

The internet has transformed many areas of business, especially the automotive sector. Everyone likes to shop around when they buy a vehicle, and automotive websites have become a key destination for consumers looking for their next vehicle. The internet has made finding the right vehicle easier for the buyer, with sophisticated search forms enabling buyers to quickly find the vehicle of their choice. In all, over 4.1 million people sourced vehicles online in 2005 (Source: Q1/Q2 2005 BRMB). This represents a 20% increase compared to the same period in 2004.

A wide range of sites have launched catering for this growing demand, including Jamjar.com, Oneswoop and Virgincars. However, autotrader.co.uk – already a major brand in offline car sales – is the biggest player in the market, being the UK's number one motoring website for new and used cars and one of the top 16 most-viewed sites in the UK (Source: Hitwise February 2005).

The automotive market is also the one of the most popular areas of classified advertising on the internet, beating other popular areas, including entertainment, media and leisure. According to Hitwise, autotrader.co.uk enjoys a 38% share of the entire market for online classified ads.

Achievements

Since its inception nine years ago, autotrader.co.uk has become a big player in the online automotive industry. In October 2005, the site attracted 4.8 million unique users, and generated 50.3 million vehicle searches. Between the months January and October 2005, consumers carried out over half a billion vehicle searches on autotrader.co.uk. It now stands as Europe's largest motoring website. As a result, it has not only

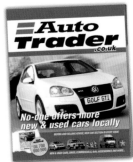

become the UK's biggest online showroom for consumers, but also a major destination for advertisers. With so many valuable visitors attracted to it, autotrader.co.uk is at the forefront of the online advertising boom, helping to fuel a market that grew by a further 62% in 2005 (Source: IAB 2005).

The explosion of the online brand is part of a wider success story. The Auto Trader magazine, with 13 regional editions, has grown into the biggest motoring magazine, with a readership of over 1.75 million per week (Source: NRS 2004). It features the largest selection of new and used cars by region, than any other classified or motoring title.

When combined, Auto Trader's website, magazines, mobile and digital TV services, provide the brand with the largest captive audience of motorists in the market – a total of over 5.8 million people.

Products and Services

Auto Trader is the UK's number one destination for new and used cars, offering consumers access to its content not only through the website and the magazines, but also through mobile phones via Orange, O₂ and T Mobile. Consumers can also access Auto Trader's 'showroom' via a unique digital TV interactive offering on NTL, Telewest and Kingston Interactive Television.

Auto Trader has developed an easy-to-use, content rich website for buyers and sellers. By selecting a make and model from the dropdown fields, users can then narrow their search further and search by age, mileage, distance to travel, private or trade sale and

keyword. With over 320,000 vehicles for sale at any one time, the site enables users to get to the car they are interested in quickly.

Autotrader.co.uk also features over 26,000 new cars for sale from more than 100 providers. Auto Trader's new car search allows smaller players to compete alongside many household names, and delivers the best value deals far quicker than searching websites individually.

There is more to autotrader.co.uk than just being able to search through hundreds of thousands of vehicles. It also includes news, reviews, advice, and road tests, keeping users abreast of latest developments in the automotive world.

Personality and Goals

The Auto Trader brand is built on two major values – 'localness' and 'choice'. It aims to be the 'trusted authority' for new and used cars – both for the trade and consumers. Auto Trader has built a reputation for providing a safe marketplace for people to buy and sell cars. It aims to strengthen its positioning as market-leader in the UK and across Europe, providing innovative, leading-edge and added-value products to consumers, manufacturers, dealers, finance and insurance companies.

www.autotrader.co.uk

AVON

Market Context

Avon has provided women with opportunities for financial independence since 1886, with 4.9 million people worldwide enjoying the flexible, independent earning opportunities it offers through selling beauty products direct to customers. The UK now has 160,000 independent Avon Representatives serving around eight million customers.

Although the original door-to-door direct selling method is still a mainstay of the brand, it is the internet that has caused one of the biggest changes in Avon's history – launching the new e-Representative. Sales Representatives previously managed their business with Avon using a paper-based system, supplemented by phone and post contact; today the website and e-mail are the preferred methods of communication.

The Avon website is an essential tool to Sales Representatives – around half of whom place their orders online every three weeks. It is a bespoke business to business website, tailored to their needs within the direct selling beauty marketplace.

Avon has a huge presence in the global arena selling some 7,500 products in 143 countries. Its five largest markets in 2004 were in the US, Mexico, Brazil, UK and Japan.

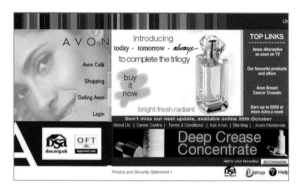

Achievements

The UK market is Avon's fourth largest, with sales topping £280 million a year – globally Avon sales total US$7.7 billion. Avon produces 60 million brochures each year, in the UK, to support 18 individual selling campaigns. During an average campaign Avon's brochure is seen by approximately six million women.

In 2003 Avon won the New Media Age award in the business to business category. It was also a finalist in the e-business 'strategy of the year' category at the 2004 National Business Awards and in the same year a finalist in the business to business category of the Biz-Net Awards.

Products and Services

Avon offers two levels of independent earnings opportunity in the UK: the well known Avon Representative and Sales Leaders who, while selling Avon products themselves, also recruit and manage their own team of Avon Representatives. The role of Sales Leader needs greater commitment to support managing the activities of a team and in return offers far greater earnings potential.

The Avon website offers Representatives, Sales Leaders and Area Sales Managers the ability to access their own accounts at any time and place customer orders in a speedy, efficient manner.

Online forums enable Representatives and Sales Leaders to chat to one another, share selling tips and provide each other with vital support.

Avon customers, and potential customers, can find out about Avon online: by browsing in the Avon Café to find out about products,

direct customers. New features include next day and two day delivery options as well as discount offers and loyalty schemes. Shoppers may also be greeted with prompts that pop up at random, offering the opportunity to shop at the discount store and purchase online bargains.

or by proceeding straight to the online shop www.avonshop.co.uk to purchase from a selection of merchandise, that ranges from cosmetics, fragrance and toiletries to lingerie and jewellery. All Avon beauty products are backed by a 100% satisfaction guarantee, giving customers additional confidence when shopping with Avon.

Customers can also keep abreast of current trends by accessing the 'What's New' service that details all the latest products.

The new UK web shop, developed as part of a global e-commerce strategy, has radically enhanced its customer services offering for

Personality and Goals

The Avon brand has built up a longstanding reputation for providing its customers with a friendly, personal service. Through product diversification and online enhancements its brand values have been updated to offer a 21st century experience. Its online personality – modern, responsive and empowering – reflects this change. Avon aims to satisfy the product service and self-fulfilment needs of women globally.

www.avon.uk.com

2003
– Bespoke website launches for Sales Leaders that enables the online management of teams.

2005
– Delivery of a new online shop, complete with an overhaul of customer logistics takes place. Avon offers overnight delivery for the first time.

bbc.co.uk
BBC

Market Context

Since 1922 the British Broadcasting Corporation (BBC) has been producing content for radio, television and most recently, the internet.

Its Public Service status defines the brand's unique identity within the marketplace. Unlike its commercial competitors the BBC funds its services through a licence-paying scheme.

As well as offering support to its successful television and radio operations, BBC websites have become destinations in their own right offering innovative, distinctive and accessible content.

In terms of unique audience bbc.co.uk currently ranks sixth in the UK behind Google, MSN, Microsoft, Yahoo! and eBay (Source: Nielsen Netview – UK home panel aged 2+ May 2005).

Achievements

Since its official launch in 1997, bbc.co.uk has dramatically expanded both its breadth of content and its reach to the UK population. It now contains over two million pages of news, sports coverage, music, science, technology and entertainment – making it the largest content site in Europe.

In the latest ABCe audit, conducted in September 2004, bbc.co.uk registered 44.8 million unique users and in June 2005 reached over half of all UK internet users (aged 15+) for the first time, with 12.9 million users (51%) out of a total internet universe of 25.6 million (Source: BBC/British Market Research Bureau (BMRB) 2005).

In 2005 the remit for bbc.co.uk was redrawn to provide stronger direction and tighter boundaries, and to ensure a clearer focus for delivering the BBC's public purposes.

Products and Services

While the BBC has helped drive internet take up with its high-quality content, bbc.co.uk is continually developing new ways for audiences to discover and enjoy this material. For instance, the websites for BBC News and BBC Sport have recently introduced Really Simple Syndication (RSS), a facility that allows users to take feeds of the BBC's own content and use it on their own sites. Valuable work has been done to extend bbc.co.uk services to mobile phones: the GCSE Bitesize Revision

World
Wide
Wonderland

service, already a successful website, is now available via mobiles, and the popular Hitchhiker's Guide to the Galaxy site was developed into a Wireless Application Protocol (WAP) service.

One of the BBC's online aspirations is to act as a trusted guide to the internet and bbc.co.uk has done worthwhile work to develop safe ways for children to explore it. CBBC Search is a family-friendly search tool that lets children search content from the CBBC website, a selection of other BBC sites and external children's websites pre-approved by the BBC.

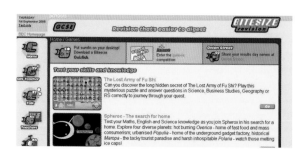

HISTORY

1994 – The BBC begins to experiment with the worldwide web, publishing a selection of programme-related content sites.

1997 – BBC Online launches trial service providing a range of programme-related sites.

1998 – Consent is granted from the Secretary of State for BBC Online.

1999 – BBC Online introduces a category system, allowing users to find content around their interests.

2000 – BBC Online joins with interactive TV to form the New Media division of the BBC.

Personality and Goals

As a Public Service brand bbc.co.uk has an obligation to increase accessibility in emerging technologies. Its brand values are inclusive, stimulating and entertaining, with a quintessentially British personality that is articulate, informed, trustworthy and educational.

The increasing take up of broadband access means that, now more than ever, the BBC can make its traditional output available in new ways; delivering compelling audio-visual content through the internet directly to its audiences. From September 2005, the BBC will trial the integrated Media Player (iMP) to a limited audience of 5,000 volunteers. iMP offers audiences the chance to catch up on the BBC's TV or Radio programmes for up to seven days after they have been transmitted, making programmes available whenever and wherever people want them.

In the coming year, bbc.co.uk will continue its work in opening up the internet to new users – particularly older people – and in providing safe content and guidance for young users.

www.bbc.co.uk

2001 – BBC Online and interactive TV services change to BBCi.

2002 – BBCi introduces its first search engine and a unique facility called Radioplayer, enabling users to catch up on radio programmes already broadcast.

2003 – iCan launches, offering a unique interactive community.

2004 – BBCi changes to bbc.co.uk after research suggests the BBCi brand is associated with interactive television.

2005 – Series of pilot schemes introduced to further increase accessibility including: RSS Feeds, Backstage and iMP Public trial.

↟ betfair.com

Market Context

Betfair operates in the burgeoning global market of 'remote' gambling, which has transformed the gaming sector, and encouraged more punters into the market.

Betfair has revolutionised the industry. Unlike traditional bookmakers, such as Ladbrokes and William Hill, Betfair allows its customers to take either side of the bet, as well as request their own odds, and bet in-play as events unfold. Betfair is a registered bookmaker operating a unique risk-free betting exchange, a model that fundamentally differs from traditional bookmakers. As Betfair's customers set the odds and amounts, Betfair takes no risk in the transaction.

The success of online gambling has created a crowded market, with over 2,400 gaming and gambling websites in the world generating over £12 billion profit in 2005 (Source: GBGC report November 2005).

Achievements

Betfair is a true pioneer of the internet age. Betfair's award-winning betting exchange engine matches up to five million bets per day, some 15 times more transactions than the London Stock Exchange, and serves over a billion page impressions per week. It is one of the most remarkable stories in internet innovation, and is one of Oracle's "four hottest databases in the world". The success of its innovation is reflected in its dominance of the betting exchange market – estimated at 90%, with over 100,000 customers betting each month.

Betfair's success has been recognised by a host of prestigious awards, including the 2003 Queen's Award for Enterprise in the Innovation category. A year earlier, the company's co-founders, former professional gambler Andrew Black, and ex-city businessman Edward Wray, were awarded the Ernst and Young Emerging Entrepreneur of the Year award. In 2004, Betfair won the CBI/Growing Business Award for 'Company of the Year', winning it again in 2005 – the first company ever to retain the award. Betfair also won the 'Editor's Choice of the Year' & 'Betting Exchange Firm of the Year' at the 2005 Inside Edge Awards.

Betfair has also set benchmarks for transparency and social responsibility. An example was its decision to launch a rescue package for customers of Sporting Options, a rival exchange that collapsed in November 2004, leaving millions of pounds of punters' money unaccounted for. This action was partly responsible for winning Betfair the Socially Responsible Operator of the Year at the 2005 e-Gaming awards. Betfair's gesture was described as "above and beyond the call of duty" by the judging panel.

Betfair's success has been matched by remarkable growth. Named in the 2005 Sunday Times Tech Track 100 as the seventh fastest growing technology company in Britain, Betfair has grown from a handful of employees in November 1999 to 620 employees in November 2005. It has also rapidly expanded its offering, launching an online poker room and a set of innovative exchange-based games. One of the fastest-growing poker rooms on the internet in 2004/05, Betfair Poker now has over 60,000 registered players, and has ambitions to be the largest poker room in the world.

Products and Services

The heart of Betfair's service is its pioneering exchange betting concept, allowing members to bet against each other rather than a traditional bookmaker. The fundamental benefit of this is that it allows a punter to take an opinion that a team or an individual horse would either win or not win, and bet accordingly. This provides considerably

HISTORY

2000 – The Sporting Exchange Ltd launches Betfair.com from its offices in Russell Square, London.

2001 – Betfair matches £1 million in seven days for the first time.

2002 – Betfair announces a merger with competitor Flutter.com, as well as its sponsorship of Fulham Football Club.

2003 – Betfair wins Queen's Award for Enterprise, in the Innovation category.

better value to the punter, as there is no bookmaker building in a margin to his price.

Betfair's in-play betting allows punters to match bets between themselves in real-time, as a football match unfolds, or even until a horse crosses the line.

The site itself is a bustling global marketplace of betting and interaction. Betfair's forum allows its members to discuss whatever takes their interest and attracts over 10,000 messages a day. Betfair also plans to provide an increasing amount of interactive gambling content, including stats, form, results, opinion and previews of many of the events the company covers.

The most recent additions to the Betfair product are Exchange Poker and Exchange Blackjack. The rapid success of these has prompted Betfair to unveil a new suite of products to challenge the established gaming market. Betfair Games are based on the company's exchange platform, but allow punters to bet on automated events such as a hand of poker or a game of blackjack. Already immensely popular, these could revolutionise the gaming market in the same way as Betfair has invigorated sports betting.

Personality and Goals

Betfair stands for value, choice, fairness, integrity, and transparency. The company also welcomes winning customers and takes no position in the markets it operates. It merely opens, manages and then settles the markets once the result is known. This is a stance that has prompted Betfair to lead the way in the drive for transparency in sport and gambling.

These qualities have been demonstrated in Betfair signing 16 Memoranda of Understanding with various sporting bodies around the world including UEFA and the Jockey Club. These are information-sharing agreements which are designed to help in the fight against corruption in sport, allowing sporting bodies unprecedented access to betting records.

Equally Betfair stands for outstanding technical excellence and innovation in the online world. It employs some of the sharpest minds in technology, attracted by the opportunity to work on a ground-breaking and award-winning site.

www.betfair.com

2004 – Betfair launches Betfairpoker.com and hosts its first online poker tournament with £100,000 prize money.

2005 – Betfair announces Channel 4 Ashes 2005 cricket broadcast sponsorship and is granted a license in Austria, its first outside the UK. Exchange Poker launches, combining its exchange platform and poker product. Furthermore, Betfair records the highest-ever single-market turnover, matching £36 million on the fifth Ashes Test match.

BoysStuff.co.uk
serious fun

Market Context

Although relatively young, the gadgets and toys sector has become fiercely competitive, and being first to market with a major product can be crucial, particularly in the key fourth quarter including Christmas. The demise of high-street competitors The Gadget Shop and The Discovery Store illustrates how even the biggest players in the market rely upon a constantly fresh approach and continually updated range.

Boys Stuff are the established leader in bringing cutting edge boys toys and gadgets to the online market. Several smaller UK-based competitors exist, and with relatively low start-up costs, newcomers frequently appear and disappear.

At its 1999 launch, Boys Stuff's main target customer was considered to be ABC1 males aged 18-35; 'cash rich, time poor' shoppers interested in the latest gadgets and technology at the best prices, without high street hassle. While this remains the company's core market, the expansion of the Boys Stuff product range has led to appeal amongst a wider age range. Boys Stuff's female customer base has also increased at a rapid rate, with an approximate 65% to 35% male-female split.

Achievements

In 2002 Boys Stuff was nominated for the prestigious European Catalogue and Mail Order Days (ECMOD) awards. 2003 marked the company's first win, with Boys Stuff receiving the 'Best Catalogue Makeover' award. A hat-trick of nominations was completed in 2004, with Boys Stuff winning a second award for 'Best Transactional Website'. Boys Stuff was also proud to be awarded top marks in Internet Magazine's 'Secret Shopper – Gadgets' test. Boys Stuff has also been ranked in the Top 10 best websites in the world by Internet

Magazine, and is the recipient of a five-star Award from Web User magazine, which described Boys Stuff as "by no means the only site offering this kind of gear, but probably the best".

Products and Services

Boys Stuff offers a wide and eclectic range of products that continues to grow and evolve. Items such as the La-z Boy Massage Chair and the Slam Man 'human punchbag' have been part of the Boys Stuff

HISTORY

1997 – The Boys Stuff concept is born out of sheer frustration at the lack of unusual, innovative, and above all fun gifts for adult males.

1999 – The idea comes to fruition with the company launching as a subsidiary of Advantage Holdings Ltd, with what founder Richard North describes as 'three people in a tiny room with no windows or air conditioning'.

2001 – Boys Stuff moves to dedicated premises.

range from day one and are now synonymous with the brand, while other fashion-led items with heavy media coverage enjoy short, intense periods of high sales. The traditional desktop toys, pocket gadgets and novelties range has expanded to include a wide selection of MP3 players, digital cameras, GPS road safety and navigation systems and hobbyist ranges such as MiniMoto bikes, power kites and boards. A key aim of Boys Stuff is to give customers the chance to own the latest 'must-have' product first and at the best price.

Unhappy at the way existing back-end systems were slowing down order completion and delivery time, Boys Stuff invented its own system, ePandora®, now in use since 2002. ePandora® has not only dramatically reduced order-processing time, but also gives customers up-to-date stock information, with automatic updates every 60 seconds and the option to track orders.

Personality and Goals

A concept key to the Boys Stuff ethos is that customers should be treated like people, not order numbers. Boys Stuff does not use an external customer service centre, and all its advisors are based in-house, so they receive product training, giving them a knowledge they can pass on to the customer.

At the heart of the Boys Stuff brand is a commitment to customer involvement, with irreverent humour used to create a strong brand identity. Boys Stuff customers respond positively to genuine enthusiasm for the products. Even complaints are dealt with using a healthy dose of fun, with tongue-in-cheek threats that the boss will shoot anyone responsible for mistakes.

www.boysstuff.co.uk

2002 – Boys Stuff and its former parent company Advantage Holdings Ltd merge to create the Brand Advantage Group (BAG).

2003 – Boys Stuff undergoes a tenfold increase in permanent staff, before a further move to accommodate rapid growth.

2003 – Boys Stuff wins prestigious ECMOD award for 'Best Catalogue Makeover'.

2004 – Boys Stuff wins ECMOD award for 'Best Transactional Website'.

Market Context

The British Airways London Eye is a 21st century symbol for Britain that provides a unique and inspiring experience offering spectacular views, bold and stylish design and a central location. The London Eye stands for the best of British architecture, innovation and engineering; instils a quiet pride and passion in its citizens, awe and amazement in all visitors. Today, the London Eye has become, quite literally, the way the world sees London. Yet it was conceived, designed and built against considerable odds. The London Eye company has three equal shareholders, British Airways, Marks Barfield Architects, creators of the London Eye and The Tussauds Group, Europe's leading operator of visitor attractions, which operates the wheel.

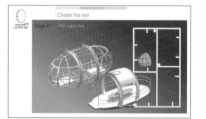

Achievements

Since opening in 2000, the British Airways London Eye has won numerous awards for tourism, architecture and engineering. The London Eye is the most popular paid-for visitor attraction in Britain.

www.ba-londoneye.com now receives in excess of 110,000 unique visitors every month. It was awarded Tourism Website of the Year Gold Award 2004 by the Excellence in England Tourism Award. It also received two awards presented by the Marketing Communication Consultants Association (MCCA) in association with Joshua Agency: the Best Photography Award 2004 and the Best Art Direction for Advertising Communications Award 2004.

The website was awarded Visit Britain's Excellence in England, Gold Award, Tourism Website of the Year 2004. The organisation called the site 'impressive' saying it 'shows great innovation'. It also recognised the site's 'outstanding design and innovative technology with an insistence on getting the important basics right'.

Products and Services

At 135m, the British Airways London Eye is the world's tallest observation wheel, with 40km panoramic views on a clear day. The gradual flight in one of the 32 high-tech glass capsules takes approximately 30 minutes offering spectacular views of London and its famous landmarks such as Big Ben, Buckingham Palace and St Paul's Cathedral.

HISTORY

1993 – Husband and wife architects David Marks and Julia Barfield conceive the idea and created the first drawings of the London Eye.

1998 – London Eye construction begins (the total construction time was 16 months).

1999 – The wheel is raised into position on the South Bank.

January 1st 2000 – The attraction is formally launched on Millennium Eve by the Prime Minister, Tony Blair.

March 8th 200 – The London Eye open to the public for the first commercial flights.

The 'Fast Track' check-in provided after booking at www.ba-londoneye.com allows guests to check in 15 minutes before their flight, enjoy fast-track entry, priority boarding and a complimentary souvenir guidebook.

Looking to the future, the London Eye aims to increase its percentage of online sales, and with a new booking site recently launched, it will be the first company to allow online guests to mix and match particular ticket types.

The website provides interactive online functionality with the aim of raising its current 20% repeat visitor rate. The site encourages advance bookings through all channels, to position the London Eye as a must-see attraction, and to encourage repeat flights. It also supports traditional marketing activities. The booking engine incorporates a CRM facility that works in identifying the needs of the specific past user, and targeting them with relevant messages when they re-visit the website.

Personality and Goals

As a brand, the London Eye aims to encapsulate a distinct attitude and humour. If the London Eye was a person they would be stylish, sophisticated, relaxed, contemporary, exciting, approachable, intelligent, self-assured and cultured.

www.ba-londoneye.com

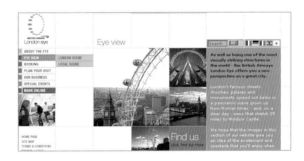

confetti
www.confetti.co.uk

may we offer you a hand in marriage?

Market Context

Approximately 300,000 couples get married in the UK every year. The average cost of a wedding is £16,000, creating an annual market of up to £5 billion. In 1999 confetti recognised the potential of the internet to harness this lucrative market, by connecting local and national businesses to prospective customers.

confetti focuses on the 25-34 year age group, early adopters of the web, who have an obsessive appetite for knowledge that is not sated by conventional media. confetti offers a definitive information service that provides multifarious options and retail opportunities to customers at influential stages in their lives.

The internet has been crucial in establishing a cost effective service both for customers and media advertisers, by helping to build up brand awareness, consumer intelligence and customer loyalty. The competitive advantage of the internet has proved invaluable in assisting confetti to create the largest database of future wedding dates in the UK, and in promoting brand expansion into new channels.

Achievements

confetti is the leading UK web destination for weddings, with no direct competitor providing a similar service. 90% of all prospective brides use confetti for help with planning their wedding.

confetti receives up to half a million unique users monthly, compared to major wedding magazine circulations which average just 50,000 every two months. confetti has been profitable since 2004 and is now a leading publisher of wedding books – having published 19 to date. By concentrating on establishing a one-stop niche service, confetti has rapidly grown in stature to become one of the largest UK female websites, delivering 13 million page impressions each month. In August 1999, just six months after its launch, confetti won the coveted title of Design Business Association's (DBA) best corporate design. In October of the same year it won two Institute of Practioners in Advertising (IPA) awards for press and radio advertising.

Products and Services

confetti provides consumers with an efficient, user-friendly, one-stop information and retail service for planning weddings and other life-

GROOM

2 563200 237820

(unfortunately that's one thing we don't stock at our wedding shop)

enhancing occasions. It uses multi-channel propositions to display retail opportunities and offer guidance and advice. confetti.co.uk has 12 online channels covering a variety of related subjects. These include: honeymoons, venues, fashion, as well as health and beauty. Its interactive nature allows members to share ideas and converse online, via topic specific message boards. As a leading supplier of over

HISTORY

1999 – confetti.co.uk is founded by David Lethbridge and Andrew Doe and launches in early February – in time for Valentines Day.

2000 – confetti.co.uk acquires its two nearest competitors, weddingguideuk.com and webwedding.co.uk.

2000 – First confetti book is published offering a range of retail information and opportunities.

2,000 branded products, confetti uses the authority of its advice and ideas to drive sales.

confetti members can use the online catalogues and interactive website for all aspects of planning, accessing information and shopping. Each member is allotted their own file, where personal details and profiles are stored and can be edited accordingly. This can be transferred onto web pages, that enable customers to establish a personalised website where photographs, plans and other distinctive features can be posted.

confetti also provides advertisers with a cost effective way of reaching a target audience. It has become integral to the media schedule of over 800 national and local advertisers, who not only benefit from the half a million monthly unique users, but also from the 150,000 emails sent out each week to new members.

Personality and Goals

confetti is the market leader in offering advice, information and retail opportunities for commemorative events. confetti's brand values are based on positive and celebratory attributes – in keeping with its product. It is modern and fashionable but not frivolous, as illustrated by its accessible, friendly and functional website. confetti plans to use mobile technology and digital television to enhance and expand the range of services offered.

www.confetti.co.uk

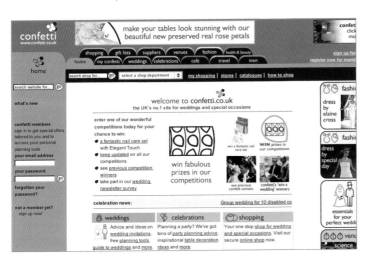

THINGS YOU DIDN'T KNOW...

confetti is addictive. Members have set up a self-help group, 'confetti anonymous', to help combat their addiction. Some users are so obsessed with planning their wedding that they log on every 30 seconds.

Graham Norton provided the voiceover for confetti's radio commercial, which won a prestigious IPA award.

38% of all confetti's website visitors are men, although women spend longer browsing and view more pages.

confetti, the movie, hits the big screen in 2006. It will be a comedy-cum-documentary based around a fictional competition that follows couples plotting the definitive wedding.

2001 – The first confetti catalogues are introduced online.

2002 – confetti expands its business to open its first retail outlet in London, selling a range of products and hosting special events.

2003 – confetti ventures into the North of England to open a shop in Leeds.

2005 – Two further stores are launched in Birmingham and Glasgow.

crocus

Market Context

The UK retail gardening sector is estimated to be worth around £4 billion per year. Unusually, for a market this size, few major brands exist nationwide. Although DIY retailers, Homebase and B&Q, sell a range of gardening equipment, they only stock a limited selection of plants. The biggest garden centre retailers, Wyevale and Dobbies, have no national presence and relatively small shares of the sector; Wyevale has a turnover of £200 million and Dobbies £55 million.

Throughout the 1990s television capitalised on the Nation's love of gardening, with programmes like Ground Force opening up the possibilities of the instant garden makeover to a newer generation of homeowners. It also boosted the market for gardening products and accessories, which grew steadily at about 15% annually – although this has recently reached a plateau.

crocus
where top garden designers get their plants
autumn 2005

Crocus was one of several horticultural e-commerce companies to recognise the potential of the market and launch in 2000. Since then all of its direct competitors have gone into administration or been bought out. The last, Gonegardening, was acquired by Crocus in 2005.

crocus
gardeners by nature

Achievements

In 2001, just one year after its launch, Crocus picked up three major awards for excellence: At the Garden Writers Guild, the gardening equivalent of the Oscars, Crocus was acclaimed the best gardening website; In the business arena The Sunday Telegraph and Barclays Bank declared Crocus the best small ecommerce business; and at the Yell.com Awards, members of the public voted Crocus the best transactional website.

HISTORY

1999 – *The embryonic idea for a gardening website is discussed and developed.*

2000 – *The Crocus website goes live.*

2000 – *A wholesale division, to supply leading designers and landscape architects, starts up.*

2001 – *Alan Titchmarsh and Charlie Dimmock, from BBC's Ground Force, join Crocus as shareholders, contributors and celebrity advisors.*

To demonstrate its ability to practice what it preaches, Crocus exhibits every year at the Chelsea Flower Show. In the last five years they have won five Gold Medals, a feat unmatched by any other company.

Products and Services

Plants are Crocus' speciality. Consumers can choose from the largest and most 'garden-worthy' range in the UK. The website is designed to be as visually stunning as the plants featured and it has a range of help and advice on all aspects of gardening. Celebrity gardener, Alan Titchmarsh, provides much of the 'How to' information and pens a regular email for everyone who signs up for his free care tips forum. For a personal consultation, consumers can send problems and queries to the Crocus 'plant doctors' who will treat all patients within 48 hours.

Customers looking for inspiration can either browse the selection of pre-designed borders or 'great combinations' Crocus has put together, or select plants to suit a 'romantic' or 'keen but clueless' gardener. For a more personal service, Crocus can offer a bespoke design. Customers can send in snaps of their garden with a few rough sketches and, in return, receive a border plan and hyperlinks to recommended plants.

Although plants are its forte, Crocus offers everything you would expect from a garden centre with one or two seasonal twists: fireworks in Autumn; Christmas trees, wreaths and gifts in Winter; and in Spring, a range of bouquets for valentines and mothers day from the Crocus florist.

Personality and Goals

Crocus is the only UK gardening website to specialise in plants. It enables users to access up to 10 times more varieties than leading conventional retailers and a wealth of expert advice through an easy-to-navigate drop down menu. As the gardener's 'knowledgeable friend', Crocus aims to demystify the technical aspects of gardening and enthuse a whole new generation of gardeners.

www.crocus.co.uk

2002 – Crocus launches its first catalogue; issue one comes out in May and issue two follows in September.

2003 – Further catalogues are launched, one to cover each season.

2005 – Crocus acquires its last remaining direct UK competitor, Gonegardening.

2005 – The compound annual growth rate for Crocus reaches 47% for the third year running.

DatingDirect.com™

Market Context

Gone are the days when internet dating was considered geeky, it is now in Vogue (literally) and in a recent poll DatingDirect.com found that 68% of people think online dating is better than its offline equivalent.

Indeed, the Western European dating market is currently worth 88 million euros and is expected to reach 352 million euros by 2009 (Source: Jupiter). Revenues of the leading European dating websites are expected to more than double over the next five years, from US$200 million to US$450 million, with the UK online dating market showing a massive boost in terms of revenue (Source: Jupiter).

Online dating is particularly popular with people in the 25-34 age bracket, who account for one-third of online dating users, while research has also suggested that the use of online dating with the 55+ age group is growing (Source: Consumer Intelligence).

Achievements

DatingDirect.com is the market leader and attracts a staggering 579,000 unique users a month, when compared to its closest competitors, Match.com (440,000 unique users), uDate.com (384,000 unique users) and Yahoo! Personals (491,000 unique users) (Source: Nielsen// NetRatings).

Darren Richards, co-founder of DatingDirect, was featured as one of the UK's top 100 entrepreneurs in The Sunday Times. Furthermore, in 2004, DatingDirect was ranked number 35 in The Sunday Times/Microsoft Tech Track 100. In addition, DatingDirect.com has not only grown its business successfully, but has also almost doubled its membership in one year.

Products and Services

DatingDirect.com is a serious site for people looking for genuine relationships. DatingDirect.com's unique selling point is that it makes online dating easy, with no gimmicks or complicated procedures. Users simply complete a short, online profile. They then select the age range and then the area that they want their potential partner to come from. Every profile and photo is checked thoroughly by DatingDirect.com's customer service team to ensure that users are genuinely looking for a relationship.

Find love online with DatingDirect.com

Join now and receive a free trial membership worth £4.95

DatingDirect.com is the UK's largest dating service, with over 3 million members. There's no joining fee, full membership starts from as little as five pounds and you're always in control.

If you're serious about looking for a relationship, go direct to www.datingdirect.com

Get 3 days free trial worth £4.95 and contact other singles when you join for free!

How to claim
Go to www.datingdirect.com and join the website for free. Once your profile has been approved click the Promotional Code link at the bottom of the Members Homepage. Enter the code NDF324 when prompted.

This offer is open to new UK members of DatingDirect.com and can only be used once. Offer expires 31st August 2005. This offer is based on your dating profile being accepted as stated in our website Terms and Conditions. No cash alternative is available. DatingDirect.com reserves the right to refuse membership.

Since its launch in 1999, DatingDirect.com has provided unlimited opportunities for members to meet like-minded people. Whether members are UK based, oversees, or even just around the corner, through DatingDirect.com they all have a very real opportunity of finding love online. As part of its value-added online offering, users have the option of using a convenient SMS mobile alert service, which makes them aware of new messages in their inbox.

Rather than a chat environment or personals/classified service, DatingDirect.com is a respectable dating service for singles looking for serious friendships and relationships, cutting out the expensive introduction fees of traditional agencies, which are now in decline.

Personality and Goals

DatingDirect.com is a site for people looking for genuine relationships – the site and personality of the brand reflects this. It is a non-gimmicky site, with no pop ups or advertising. It really is all about dating and giving members exactly what they want. DatingDirect.com believes in staying true to its objective of providing members with a quality, hassle-free experience.

Safety and security is very important to how DatingDirect.com operates and it keeps these factors at the heart of its proposition. Its core member base is made up of busy professionals between 25-45 years old. Working hard can leave little time to look for love and DatingDirect.com's aim is to provide the perfect environment for these people to meet thousands of potential dates in a fun, safe and secure way.

www.datingdirect.com

THINGS YOU DIDN'T KNOW...

Members send more than two million messages via the website every week – that's three messages every second.

DatingDirect.com receives thousands of emails from couples that have found love via its service. One such couple, Darren and Jenny, whose date went well didn't realise just how close they lived to each other until they shared a taxi home – their houses were less than a hundred metres apart.

More than 5,000 new members join the DatingDirect.com service per day.

2003 – DatingDirect.com has just over one million active users. This year sees the 'birth' of National Dating Day, which is created to encourage busy, professional Britons to celebrate dating and relationships.

2004 – DatingDirect.com embarks on providing exclusive dating services to some of the UK's most recognised and respected brands, including AOL.co.uk, GMTV.com, ITV.com, Channel4.com, Tiscali.co.uk and Handbag.com.

2005 – DatingDirect.com now boasts over three million members.

dubit

Market Context

There are 4.84 million young people aged between 11 and 17 in the UK with over one in five of the current population under 16 years of age. Of the 11-17 year-olds 93% regularly surf the internet – surpassing those who watch television (91%) – for an average of 4.8 hours per day (Source: Dubit Research 2005).

With teenage disposable income totalling over £16 billion annually and 85% buying on impulse – predominantly with their own money (only 30% comes from parents, most is earned through part-time jobs) – the internet provides unlimited opportunities for marketing in the teenage spending sector.

Recognising that a main factor to online success is an effective interface that teenagers can buy into, and through using its unique insight into the target market, Dubit harnesses the latest technologies and delivers solutions. Teenagers are early adopters of new technologies and Dubit aims to keep ahead of the market.

Achievements

Since its launch www.dubit.co.uk has grown – mainly through word of mouth – to provide a chat service for over 300,000 young people.

In 2001 Dubit received a special commendation in the E-Commerce Awards, it was also nominated in the same year for a Yell.com award and a BAFTA award for interactivity.

Dubit is the pioneer of virtual 3D focus groups. New technology enables online focus groups to operate like a chat room, with young people invited to attend via email.

Through working with leading brands and public sector clients, such as Sky Sports and The British Museum, Dubit creates meaningful online spaces for young people. For instance, in a recent collaboration with West Yorkshire Police, Dubit produced a CD Rom that teaches young people about citizenship in a fun and playful way.

Dubit contributes to the Home Office Internet Taskforce on Child Protection – which has developed guidelines for all chat sites – and in 2005 was awarded best public sector service project online for 'The Child Protection on the Internet Campaign' (commissioned by i-Level).

Products and Services

Dubit is a youth research and communications agency that incorporates the youth portal www.dubit.co.uk and DubitCard.

Dubit used the UK's first 3D chat room technology to create www.dubit.co.uk – an online community for UK teenagers. One of the site's main attractions is the 3D cartoon world where teenagers can create their own avatar.

Dubit also offers the only personalised VIP and discount card for 11-17 year olds in the UK, DubitCard, enabling users to benefit from discounts when purchasing goods on and offline through leading retailers. Partners include Vue Cinema, Pizza Hut, UKClubculture and The Dungeons, with plans afoot to incorporate a payment mechanism through linking the card to a banking sector.

Youth Research is at the heart of the Dubit organisation, it owns and runs the UK's largest online youth research panel – Informer. Over 30,000 young people aged between seven and 24 are opted in to take part in research, enabling Dubit to conduct

HISTORY

1999 – Dubit is set up by eight young people with the aim of revolutionising youth marketing by changing it around to actively engage the consumer.

2000 – www.dubit.co.uk launches as a youth shopping site offering mobile phones and other gadgets.

2001 – Insider Street Teams are established across the UK.

Eight teenagers, who felt that youth marketing was condescending and missing the mark, founded Dubit as a company that spoke directly to young people. It generated strategies that connected on a deeper level with what they knew about the youth market.

Dubit entered the Guinness Book of Records in 2000 as the Youngest Limited Company in the UK, with the youngest director aged just 13 years old.

cost-effective online surveys and focus groups, quickly and with valid and accurate responses.

Dubit has an outstanding reputation for innovative online campaigns as well as a unique, credible and reliable youth insight through its research department. The research extends across a vast range of topic areas and clients, in both private and public sectors.

Dubit Interactive develops and integrates e-solutions for both public and private sector industries and since its inception has been instrumental in maintaining the safety of its chat site by campaigning for safe protected areas.

Personality and Goals

Dubit creates innovative spaces and projects where teenagers can feel valued and understood. Dubit's brand values are built around youth, opportunity and progress. Through believing and investing in young people Dubit has built up a brand that fosters trust. Its personality mirrors the archetypal teenager: youthful, individual, confident and responsive while encouraging users to seek out new experiences and explore their environment.

www.dubitlimited.com

2002 – Research & Interactive Divisions of www.dubitlimited.com are created.

2003 – The DubitCard launches giving users the opportunity to benefit from product discounts with recognised card partners such as Pizza Hut and Vue Cinema.

2005 – Dubit expands its research & strategy divisions to become market leaders in the youth arena.

Market Context

As an early internet enthusiast, eBay founder, Pierre Omidyar, was quick to identify the potential for a central location where customers could trade an assortment of items and meet other users with similar interests.

You can't lose when you sell your car on eBay Motors.

It's easy. You set a minimum price for your car and potential buyers start the bidding from there. You can't lose because there's never any chance of being haggled down. Of course you could really win and sell your car for more than you imagined. And because you can set a reserve price, you never have to sell for less than you want. It costs from just £6 to list your car on eBay Motors, so go on, get lucky.

buy it. sell it. love it. **ebaY** Motors™

www.ebaymotors.co.uk

Today eBay is the world's biggest online marketplace with a global customer base of 157 million and a global presence in 33 markets. Since its launch it has created an unrivalled market for the sale of goods and services by a passionate community of individuals and small businesses.

eBay.co.uk was launched in October 1999, and is undisputedly the UK's largest online market place and number one e-commerce site (Source: Nielsen//NetRatings May 2003). It currently registers approximately three million live listings, meaning there are approximately three million items for sale on the site at any one time.

Achievements

In February 2005 eBay.co.uk hit the 10 million user milestone for the first time, with every third internet user recorded as visiting the site at least once every month (Source: Nielsen//NetRatings April 2005). By August 2005 this audience had increased to 1.2 million.

During the same month, eBay.co.uk's reach of the market was 43% – where reach is the percentage of all active internet users within that month visiting the site. eBay.co.uk now offers over 13,000 categories, with new and used items ranging from collectibles; like trading cards, antiques, and dolls to practical items; like used cars, clothing, books and electronics.

eBay.co.uk accounts for 10% of the total time UK users spend on the internet (Source: Nielsen//NetRatings April 2005), with site visitors spending a monthly average of one hour 54 minutes online viewing some 280 pages.

In 2004, gross merchandise volume (GMV) – the value of all successfully closed listings on eBay.co.uk – reached a record US$3.7 billion and eBay.co.uk reported a year-over-year GMV growth of 94%.

The eBay.co.uk market continues to grow at a strong rate, and in that process reached an important milestone in 2005: its first ever US$100 million revenue quarter.

Products and Services

On an average day millions of items are listed on eBay.co.uk. Users visit to buy and sell items in over 13,000 categories, with buyers given the option to purchase either in an auction-style format or at a fixed price, through a feature called 'Buy It Now'.

HISTORY

1995 – Founder, Pierre Omidyar, launches eBay as the world's first online marketplace.

1999 – eBay.co.uk launches as the UK's first online marketplace.

2002 – eBay acquires PayPal – previously the payment method of choice by over 50% of eBay users.

2004 – Gross merchandise volume (GMV) – the value of all successfully closed listings on eBay.co.uk – reaches a record US$3.7 billion.

eBay.co.uk offers a wide variety of educational tools, features, and services that enable members to buy and sell on the site quickly, safely, and conveniently. These include online payments through PayPal, tips on safe trading, and the Developers Programme for community members who aspire to develop unique technology solutions.

To help the community trade safely and build trust with one another eBay.co.uk, like other eBay sites, offers a range of tools, programmes and resources. For instance, Feedback, where through positive, negative and neutral ratings and comments each eBay member accrues a feedback score. All sellers display this score in the seller information box on the item listings page, similar to walking into a high street store and finding the previous 10 customers have written up their shopping experience on the wall.

Feedback fosters trust between users by acting as both an incentive to do the right thing and as a mark of distinction for those who conduct transactions with respect, honesty and fairness.

Personality and Goals

Rooted in the values of the marketplace, eBay's brand values are aimed at offering a level playing field: encouraging open, honest, and accountable transactions, and creating economic opportunities for everyone.

It has an unpretentious, friendly and upbeat personality that appeals to a global audience through its core values of transparency and trust.

www.eBay.co.uk

2005 – eBay acquires Gumtree, a network of UK local city classifieds sites.

2005 – eBay.co.uk hits the 10 million user milestone for the first time.

2005 – Second quarter figures show eBay.co.uk's audience has grown to 11.2 million (Source: Nielsen//NetRatings August 2005).

2005 – On average, eBay.co.uk's reach of the UK internet market hits 43% within any given month (Source: Nielsen//NetRatings August 2005).

Market Context

With a 21.81% share of the market, Faceparty is the leading online community of its kind in the UK (Source: Hitwise). Its closest competitor has a market share of just 2.25%, making Faceparty almost 10 times more popular than any other product in its category (Source: Hitwise).

Faceparty is used primarily by 16-24 year olds throughout the UK and although its users are all ages, 52% fall into the 16-19 age group. One out of every 61 visitors to the Faceparty site add it to their list of favourites, and an average session at the site is 20 minutes and nine seconds, which is above the average of 12 minutes and 41 seconds in the online community category (Source: Hitwise).

Achievements

Since its launch in June 2000, Faceparty has attracted more than 5,000,000 audited UK subscribers and continues to attract an additional 35,000 new members every week (Source: ABC Electronic). Furthermore, by March 2005 Faceparty.com had achieved 1.5 billion page impressions per month.

The company prides itself on its innovative drive, having been the first global website to ever offer photo-uploads direct from mobile phones and having beat MSN and Yahoo! to the creation of software free-instant messaging by over three years.

Faceparty is also proud that it set the global standard in the way that children are protected from adult content in chat-rooms. Indeed, since it is near impossible for a child to come into contact with adult content on Faceparty, the Internet Watch Foundation uses Faceparty

HISTORY

June 2000 – Faceparty.com opens its doors. Within three months there are 5,000 members, all down to word of mouth.

September 2002 – Faceparty launches its events arm, with a 7,000 capacity launch party. Three years and 12 events later, Faceparty is a creative leader in the events industry.

as a case study for others, such as AOL or Google, to follow.

Products and Services

Faceparty was the world's first ever web-based community to combine profiles, photo-sharing, online messaging and chat for the very first time. Cutting-edge products allow members to search for one another in their area, upload and edit their pictures, design their own personal 'profiles' (a kind of social CV) or to use the 'undercover agent' to find out which members have secret crushes on them.

Faceparty knows everything about its individual users: what they listen to, what they ate for dinner last night, where they last went on holiday, making it a powerful youth marketing tool. Regular advertisers with Faceparty include Coca-Cola, Sony, Tesco and Virgin.

But Faceparty does not only exist online; it is also a leading party organiser. Indeed, Faceparty events have been heralded as the best in the world by leading opinion formers such as the editors of MixMag and FHM. For one event, Faceparty took over a warehouse complex, where it built a rainforest, complete with more than 10,000 real plants and trees, huge artificial lakes and a giant waterfall. Beneath the waterfall stood a secret cave, where Aphex Twin and guests performed to those who discovered it. Faceparty's events have attracted audiences in excess of 35,000 people.

Personality and Goals

The Faceparty brand, with its tagline 'The biggest party on earth' is about people, being young, living wild and going to awesome parties.

The company is currently laying foundations for long-term goals. Negotiations are in place to help extend the brand into new markets. As well as remaining at the cutting-edge of communicative and interactive web development, the Faceparty youth entertainment brand aims to expand through radio, downloads, nightclubs, festivals and TV. For example, Faceparty is in development with a large broadcaster for a new daily TV show.

www.faceparty.com

April 2003 – *Faceparty celebrates reaching 1,000,000 members. The 1,000,000th member was flown from Leeds to London, where they were greeted by Jordan, Bez, Shaun Ryder, Goldie, George & Zippy from Rainbow and Grim Rita for a private dinner on the roof of a sky-scraper.*

December 2004 – *The full-time Faceparty team has grown from three employees in 2000 to a total of 40.*

September 2005 – *Faceparty becomes the single largest UK owned global website, by page impression.*

firebox.com

Market Context

Over the past decade the internet has developed into a viable, secure shopping channel. In 1995 there were 56 million internet users worldwide, and global e-retail sales were less than US$300 million. By 2004, the internet was a mainstream shopping channel generating £14.5 billion worth of revenue in the UK alone (Source: IMRG eRetail Annual Report, 2005).

Simultaneously, the gifts and gadgets retail sector has come of age. Firebox was set up to tap into the adult segment – where buyers are looking to purchase interesting and unusual products. Online retailing offers substantially lower barriers to entry and so competitors such as I Want One of Those and Boys Stuff soon followed.

With the profile of the gadget sector growing and stealing share from traditional gift outlets, many high-street retailers entered the sector, including Argos, John Lewis, Marks & Spencer and Next. However, operating online has meant that companies such as Firebox can act much more quickly than high street competitors.

To stay ahead of its online competition, Firebox has been prolific in securing a number of UK-first and exclusive product launches,

including the Atari Classics Plug & Play TV Game, Gupi, Phobile, 20Q Mind Reader, Shinco Portable DVD range, TV Wristwatch, Perplex City, Pino, Doggles and many more.

Achievements

Established in 1998, Firebox is one of the UK's leading multi-channel retailers. It has been profitable since late 2001 and has grown very rapidly. Turnover for 2004 was £8 million, and Firebox was ranked as the 13th fastest-growing business in the UK (Source: Sunday Times FastTrack 100, 2004).

Firebox sources products from around the world in order to identify the 'next big thing'. Indeed, many major high street retailers

HISTORY

1993 – *Michael Smith and Tom Boardman meet at Birmingham University and make a pact to start a business after leaving full-time education.*

1998 – *Hotbox.co.uk, a place to buy cool stuff, is born; Michael and Tom operate the company out of Tom's parents' attic in Cardiff.*

1998 – *Michael and Tom create their first product – the Shot Glass Chess Set, which catapultes the company into public recognition.*

1999 – *The company receives seed funding from New Media Spark and move to new offices in London.*

watch Firebox to identify products that will go on to become successful in the mass market. In 2004, the company shipped 175,000 orders.

Firebox.com receives 4.5 million monthly page impressions and attracts 680,000 monthly users (Source: Nielsen//NetRatings).

In 2005 the company was a finalist at the Retail Week Awards and was named in the Real Business Hot 100 and as one of the Top 100 Fastest Growing UK Businesses 2001-2004.

Products and Services

Firebox.com sources unique, unusual and quirky products from around the world – appealing to buyers looking for gifts that are original and different. It strives to be first to market with brand new products, spotting the next big thing and bringing it to its customers long before its competitors.

More than a simple buying opportunity, Firebox aims to provide customers with interesting, amusing and informative reviews, allowing more information on products than high street stores can manage. The company believes that high-level customer support, excellent online security and stress-free fulfillment, draws consumers to its brand.

Personality and Goals

The Firebox concept is that "...you don't stop playing when you get old, you get old when you stop playing".

Firebox ultimately aims to deliver fun and so the brand personality has been shaped to reflect this. Everything from the way that the customer service team interacts with customers to the vibrant office atmosphere, the 'Playing with Fire' club nights and the free bag of retro sweets included with every order are all designed to convey the feelings of fun, youthfulness, excitement and passion about what Firebox does.

www.firebox.com

April 2000 – The business changes its name from Hotbox.co.uk to Firebox.com.

2000 – Firebox strikes a deal with Endemol to be one of the e-commerce sponsors for the first UK Big Brother TV Show.

2003 – Firebox launches the first of its Playing with Fire club nights in Central London.

2004 – Heading into a record-breaking Christmas sales period for the business, Firebox.com features at number 13 in the Sunday Times Fast Track 100.

2005 – Firebox announces an on-pack promotion with leading beer brand Carling.

Market Context

Friends Reunited was born out of the dotcom boom of the late 1990s, when entrepreneurs chased the new media goldrush. Many were backed by venture capitalists, others were launched from back bedrooms. Only a few survived. One of those was Friends Reunited. Harnessing the power of the internet to people's desire to rediscover lost friendships and share nostalgic memories, Friends Reunited created a new market in internet business, and in doing so, opened up new avenues for expansion. Whether it is finding old colleagues, school friends or neighbours or tracing family trees, there is an insatiable desire from people all over the world to reconnect with their past – and the internet is the ideal medium.

Achievements

From its humble beginnings, Friends Reunited has not only become one of the most successful dotcom brands, but also a cultural phenomenon. It has changed thousands of lives, helping people rediscover old friends and colleagues, find romance and trace their roots.

The speed with which Friends Reunited took off shows how it tapped into a vast unmet demand. With 3,000 members by the end of 2000, one million by August 2001 and 12 million in 2005, Friends Reunited grew through word of mouth, attracting massive media interest in the process. It inspired a BBC TV game show

called 'Class Of…' which brought together old classmates, while ITV also introduced a show based on the site, 'With a Little Help from my Friends'. In 2001 the Steve Wright Radio 2 show nominates Friends Reunited 'Website of the Day', prompting tens of thousands of listeners to log on. By August the site had one million members.

Its success has been recognised through various awards, being voted amongst the Top 10 Most Influential Sites Ever (Source: Nielsen 2003) and winning Most Promising Young Company (Source: CBI December 2003). Friends Reunited was also awarded No 1 Digital Brand in the UK (Source: NOP September 2003).

Products and Services

The core premise of Friends Reunited is getting in touch with old friends whether they are school friends, work mates, forces colleagues,

club members or neighbours. The site also offers members the chance to exchange memories and reminisce on the message boards.

Thanks to the formation of an international database, merging sites in Australia, New Zealand and South Africa, members of Friends Reunited can now search for friends across the globe all from the one site.

Genes Reunited is now the UK's largest family tree, genealogy and ancestry site, with four million members and over 40 million relations listed worldwide. 'Cyber detectives' can use the site to unlock the secrets in their family tree. It is free to join and search, with an annual fee to make contact with other members.

HISTORY

1999 – Julie Pankhurst, was curious what her old school friends were up to. She urges database programmer husband Steve to develop a website to help connect old friends.

2000 – Friends Reunited is officially launched in July 2000, from the back bedroom of the Pankhurst's house in Barnet, London. By the end of the year it had 3,000 registered members.

2002 – Friends Reunited starts the year with [four million members and ends it with over eig million. Workplaces Reunited is launched and August the first Friends Reunited baby was bor

Friends Reunited Dating, which is not for dating your old school friends, has over 400,000 dating members. The care taken managing the content of member profiles ensures it remains a respectable site for singles of all ages. It is free to register and view potential partners online with a fee for making contact with other members.

Also in 2003, the first Friends Reunited CD, an 80s compilation, hit the shops and went gold, selling over 100,000 copies. This was followed by compilations for the 90s, 50s, 60s and 70s.

Friends Reunited Jobs allows members to sort vacancies by category, location and wage for free, and also allows companies to post vacancies and search for candidates. The site helps jobseekers get headhunted, and because it's completely confidential, people have nothing to lose by registering.

The company's latest addition, Friends Connections, helps link people with similar interests, both local and global. If you're into model railways or maybe just want to find a new tennis partner, the site will find fellow enthusiasts.

Personality and Goals

Having been conceived by a husband and wife team in the back bedroom of a London semi, Friends Reunited has always been friendly, unpretentious and approachable. Its success is based on the simple desire to stay in touch with old friends and its vision is to help people make connections, enjoy good company, discover more about themselves and their past. The company never forgets that its success is down to its members – they form the community that gives Friends Reunited its strength and value.

www.friendsreunited.co.uk

2003 – A new management team is appointed – Michael Murphy as CEO, Rob Mogford as CFO and Tim Ward as Marketing Director.

2004 – Friends Reunited makes its first acquisition, buying schoolfriends.co.uk, a key competitor in Australia. Genes Connected, introduced in 2002, changes its name to Genes Reunited. By the end of the year it has tripled its membership to 2.3 million with close to 30 million names listed.

2005 – Friends Connections is launched, the company acquires the online jobsboard Top Dog Jobs and Friends Reunited Jobs is launched.

Google

Market Context

Search engines are at the front line of internet usage. In many ways they are what binds the internet together, aggregating information into a manageable, useful serving – available in a split second.

Given that nearly every internet user uses a search engine, the traffic passing though them is enormous – and the competition between them intense. Google™ is the leader of the pack. The service that was started in a garage by two students has grown to overtake Yahoo! and Microsoft to become the most popular search engine in the world. In the UK, over 14 million people use it every month – roughly three times as many as its next closest rival MSN Search (5.1 million) and Yahoo! (4.2 million) (Source: Nielsen//Net Ratings December 2004).

Last year, Microsoft launched a bid to take on Google's leading position, unveiling MSN Search, backing it with a high profile marketing campaign.

A key attraction for any player in this market is to grab a slice of the increasingly lucrative search engine marketing revenue. According to the Interactive Advertising Bureau, £250 million was spent on search engine marketing in 2004.

Achievements

Google's growth has been meteoric, overtaking the web's biggest guns to become the world's most popular search engine in just seven years. It is a formidable tool, returning results from eight billion

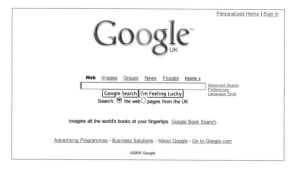

indexed web pages, two billion images and one billion usenet messages in a fraction of a second. Every month 380 million unique users around the world take advantage of its services (Source: Nielsen//NetRatings August 2005). No wonder its fans say that Google is the 'web's ultimate answer machine'. Its name has even entered the vernacular as a verb with people often saying, "I'll Google it".

Google's success has been built on the strength of its product, gaining reputation, scale and fame by word of mouth. The enthusiasm of its users has done what others invest millions in marketing to achieve.

Technically, Google has always been ahead of the field. When others assumed large servers were the fastest way to handle massive amounts of data, Google blazed a new trail and found networked PCs to be faster. When its rivals accepted apparent speed limits imposed by search algorithms, Google wrote new algorithms that proved there were no limits.

The company has kept true to its founding principles. It is a commercial, profitable company, but keeps its interface and user experience uncluttered by advertising messages or other distractions. It is a pure and democratic view that has won the hearts of internet users all over the world.

HISTORY

1995 – Google founders Larry Page and Sergey Brin, meet at Stanford University.

1996 – Larry and Sergey collaborate on a search engine called BackRub. Buzz about the new search technology began to build as word spread around campus.

1998 – 'Google Inc' is born – its HQ a garage at a friend's house. Nevertheless, Google is already answering 10,000 search queries each day.

1999 – Google secures US$25 million funding from two leading venture capital firms in Silicon Valley.

It is now one of the world's most valuable brands, ranked at 38 in the 2005 Interbrand/Business Week Top 100 Brands survey. The Google brand is valued at US$8.4 billion, putting it above much longer established and more heavily marketed brands such as Kellogg's, GAP and Apple.

Products and Services

Four elements separate Google from its competition: speed, accuracy, objectivity and ease of use. The clean design of the site makes it abundantly clear how to proceed and offers little to distract the user in search of information. Search results are clearly separated from advertising, which is identified as 'sponsored links'.

Google's range of services is growing all the time. Spell checking, web page translation, currency conversion, calculator and a book searching function are just a few of its many capabilities. It has a comparison shopping tool, Froogle, a Google News service which scans news headlines, and tools for searching weather information, stock quotes and images. It even searches usenet messages in online chat rooms through Google Groups.

Personality and Goals

Google's goal is to provide a much higher level of service to all those who seek information. To that end, Google has persistently pursued innovation and pushed the limits of existing technology to provide a fast, accurate and easy-to-use search service that can be accessed from anywhere.

Google believes in instant gratification, responding to internet users who want immediate answers. It may be the only company in the world whose stated goal is to have users leave its website as quickly as possible.

Google's founders have often stated that the company is not serious about anything but search. They built a company around the idea that work should be challenging and the challenge should be fun. Google is now a big company, but it retains the quirkiness and idealism of its student founders, and its belief in the democratisation of information.

www.Google.co.uk

2000 – *The company moves into Googleplex, in Mountain View, California and in June becomes the world's largest search engine with its introduction of a billion-page index.*

2002 – *America Online chooses the company to provide both search and advertising to its 34 million members and tens of millions of other visitors to AOL properties.*

2004 – *Google files with the SEC for an initial public offering (IPO). In October Google announces its first quarterly results as a public company, with revenues of US$805.9 million.*

Halifax
HomeFinder
Always giving you extra

Market Context

The internet is becoming the preferred method to look for a new home. By using the web, it is now possible to easily keep up to date with what's on the market, view inside properties with high quality and even 360° images, view floor layouts and book appointments to view. For people looking to buy property overseas, or in another area of the country, the internet is especially useful, allowing users to gauge prices and quickly see what is on offer without having to visit or wait for local agents to send details. In all, the web has transformed the home-buying and renting process, empowering consumers with useful and detailed information at the click of a mouse.

For estate agents and property companies, being online has become a pre-requisite. Most have their own internet sites, but many also join the UK's four main property portals which link estate agents from all over the country: rightmove.co.uk, propertyfinder, Primelocation and findaproperty.

Although Halifax is one of the joint owners of rightmove.co.uk, it also recognised the need for an individual branded website that allowed customers to view all of its properties. This prompted it to launch HomeFinder – an exclusive site to Halifax, linking all of the homes for sale in all of its branches.

In an intensely competitive market, Halifax Estate Agents is also one of the few remaining estate agents linked to a financial institution.

Achievements

HomeFinder is now consistently one of the most viewed parts of halifax.co.uk, getting on average over 300,000 visits each month.

All of this has cemented Halifax's strength in the property market. Halifax Estate Agents is now the largest single branded estate agency in the UK. It has won numerous prestigious awards, including Best Estate Agency Chain 2005 in the Estate Agent of the Year Awards (sponsored by PSG, NAEA and the Daily Express). In addition to this, Halifax Estate Agents have won silver awards for Training & Development and Customer Service in the Estate Agency of the Year Awards 2005. It is also helping to set standards for the industry as a whole, being a founder member of the Ombudsman for Estate Agents.

HISTORY

1986 – *Halifax Estate Agencies Ltd (HEAL) is formed and acquires 12 of the UK's largest regional estate agents.*

End of 1989 – *The 12 regional companies acquire over 200 businesses in total – still trading under their regional parent company names. At its peak, this gives HEAL a 900-strong branch network.*

1990 – *Halifax Property Services launches, re-branding the majority of HEAL's offices in order to trade under a single name.*

Products and Services

The HomeFinder website was developed to be as simple as possible, with the focus on helping customers to find a home easily. With features such as the ability to download property details, access to local information via UpMyStreet and allowing customers to self register for e-mail updates of new listings, HomeFinder has become an important destination for home buyers and sellers.

The site also serves as an important tool for Halifax Estate Agents' branches, linking them all together and providing a paperless environment by storing all essential forms on the system.

HomeFinder is also used exclusively in the branches to match new properties to specific

THINGS YOU DIDN'T KNOW...

According to a HomeFinder survey, homebuyers value being near green open space more than living close to shops or other amenities.

In 2006 Halifax Estate Agents will be 20 years old.

HomeFinder has advertised 120,057 properties in the last two years, together worth £10,412,043,537.

The most expensive house it has sold was for £2,137,000. The most expensive that was ever valued was £3,500,000.

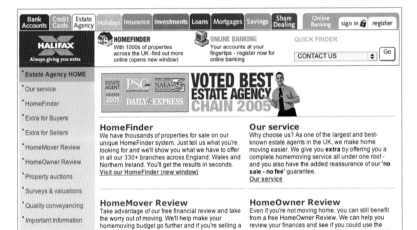

buyers' requirements. This part of HomeFinder technology is only available in branches and for buyers that have registered with Halifax Estate Agents. All buyers who use HomeFinder have quick and easy access to all Halifax financial services products, including an exclusive range of mortgages, loans, conveyancing services, and buildings and contents insurance.

Personality and Goals

Like its parent, Halifax Estate Agents, the goal of HomeFinder is to be honest and straightforward, serious about offering value, and not taking itself too seriously. It is friendly and energetic in its quest to provide 'Extra' through its people and its products. It has a clear and passionate brand promise, to 'Always give you extra'.

www.halifaxhomefinder.co.uk

2000 – Halifax Property Services becomes Halifax Estate Agents. The corporate colour is changed from red and green to the Halifax blue and the business diversifies to sell a wide range of banking and other financial services. Halifax also becomes a joint owner of rightmove.co.uk.

2002 – HomeFinder goes live on the internet in order to link all of the properties for sale with all branches to one main point and make it more accessible.

Been promoted recently?

If not, find a better job on JobServe

www.jobserve.com

Market Context

Since the introduction of job advertisements on the internet, more and more job-seekers every year turn to the web in their search to find a better job. The JobServe website advertises thousands of jobs, online, everyday on behalf of employers and agencies who have vacancies they wish to fill. These advertisers want their vacancies to be seen by a wide range of quality job-seekers and come to JobServe because of the high volume of people visiting its website everyday to view jobs within more than 15 industry-specific sectors.

Achievements

Having launched in 1993 and pioneered a 'jobs by email' service a year later, JobServe achieved record profits, and by 2000 had reached first place in the Sunday Times/ PriceWaterhouseCoopers Profit Track 100 table of the UK's most profitable companies.

The same year, it was named as Best Recruitment Website by the Recruitment & Employment Confederation (REC) in 2000, before being included in the Sunday Times/Virgin Atlantic Fast Track 100 in both 2000 and 2001.

Indeed, 2001 saw the company win the Queen's Award for Enterprise and its co-founder and managing director, Robbie Cowling, was named Ernst & Young Entrepreneur of the Year for the Central Region.

Products and Services

When advertising roles, recruiters can place advertisements containing up to 3,000 characters onto the JobServe website. Each job includes a standard online application form or, alternatively, the job-seeker can contact the recruiter directly in the usual ways.

The JobServe Job Additions service allows job advertisements to stand out from the crowd by including the option to brand, add web links or a personalised online application form for each advertisement.

These advertising opportunities provide job feeds to job-seekers by means of RSS, SMS, email, or a combination. Job-seekers can choose to receive either instant or daily notification of jobs.

Through JobServe's CV Search, recruiters can purchase a licence to search the company's extensive industry databases for job-seekers who have registered their details with JobServe. The CVs can be searched by a range of criteria including skill, geographic location or job title.

JobServe offers a range of advertising banner services. Firstly, headline advertising banners can be positioned prominently on JobServe's homepage for 24 hours and are placed at the top of

HISTORY

1993 – JobServe is formed by IT contractors Robbie Cowling and John Witney.

1994 – JobServe launches the world's first 'Jobs by Email' service and a few months later, the company launches www.jobserve.com.

1999 – JobServe unveils profits of more than £7 million from a turnover of £8.3 million.

2000 – Robbie Cowling buys out his partner John Witney.

2001 – JobServe moves into its new three-storey purpose-built offices.

its 'jobs-by-email' listing to all its subscribers for that day. Secondly, keyword sponsorship means that every time a job-seeker searches by skill, location or qualification, that has been sponsored, the advertiser's banner is displayed at the top of the results page. Finally, impressions can be purchased in blocks and appear on the top of the page and randomly across the website, except for the home page and sponsored pages.

JobServe also offers newsletter advertising, whereby every month its emailed newsletter is sent to more than 400,000 job-seekers with links to articles on JobServe. The publication contains job and industry news as well as career advice and a limited amount of selective advertising.

Personality and Goals

JobServe's advantage in being the world's first to send out job details by email was of huge benefit to a group of people – IT professionals – who had already embraced this method of communication in their everyday work lives. It proved highly viral as word spread throughout the IT community.

To ensure JobServe remains at the forefront of online recruitment advertising, the company continually seeks to innovate by introducing new services to both advertisers and job-seekers alike. Although it started out as a niche job board for IT professionals, it has now expanded across a further 14 industry sectors, with plans to grow even further.

www.jobserve.com

Market Context

Jobsite brought its brand of internet recruitment to the whole of the UK job market in 1995, with the vision of making recruitment as simple, fast and effective as possible.

In 2004 the online advertising recruitment market in the UK was valued at more than £108 million (Source: Association of Online Recruiters). When looking at candidate market share, Jobsite is the number one commercial job site (Source: Hitwise, August 2005).

Achievements

In the 10 years since it first went online, Jobsite has achieved many milestones and received countless accolades. In 2001 it became the first online recruiter operating from the UK to attract over one million visits a month. A year later, it won the Professional Recruiter Award for Excellence and the National Online Recruitment Award.

In 2003, as well as being listed as the third-fastest growing UK company by RealBusiness/Dun & Bradstreet, Jobsite won a five-year contract to provide a national online recruitment service to the nation's biggest employer, the National Health Service.

2005 was also a big year for Jobsite. The company was recognised as being one of the best companies to work for (The Sunday Times 100 Best Small Companies to Work for 2005).

Today, Jobsite has more than 2.5 million registered users and continues to develop its consumer brand.

HISTORY

1995
– Three brothers, Keith, Graham and Eric Potts, spotted a gap in the industry and took recruitment online.

1995
– Jobsite launches the UK's first multi-sector 'Jobs-by-email'.

1999
– Jobsite founds the UK internet's first professional trade body – Association of Online Recruiters.

Products and Services

Jobsite knows that different jobhunters want different things from their work-life. The site was set up to help jobhunters find what they want, whether that is to climb to the top of the career ladder or simply to find a decent job that allows them to have a well balanced life. Jobsite aims to help them search for the job that supports this balance.

Jobhunters search in different ways, so Jobsite provides a range of various search methods. As well as the ability to search by job title, sector and location, the advanced search facility allows jobhunters to search according to more specific needs.

By placing extra emphasis on understanding the obstacles faced in their job search and its impact on their lives, Jobsite stands out with its approach to jobhunters. Jobsite is able to provide not only vacancies, but useful tools such as a 'jobs by email'

service, whereby the jobhunter chooses their requirements and Jobsite delivers the relevant jobs every night straight into their email inbox. In addition, Jobsite provides value-added solutions for job hunters, such as career advice and articles, CV writing, online training courses and personality profiling. By offering these solutions, Jobsite is well-equipped to help the candidate find the right job for their lifestyle.

Attracting the right candidates with the appropriate skills and experience is key for any employer. To achieve this, Jobsite runs a targeted marketing programme focusing on candidate quality. Through strategic partnerships, Jobsite is able to provide a constant level of relevant quality candidates, filling vacancies in the shortest possible time.

THINGS YOU DIDN'T KNOW...

▌ One new job application is made by a candidate on Jobsite every 6.5 seconds.

▌ 12 new vacancies are added to Jobsite every minute of the working day.

Personality and Goals

Jobsite's ethos is to help jobhunters plan their work-life, so that their whole life works better. In order to achieve this, it endeavours to make recruitment as exciting and as painless as possible. This means that Jobsite aims to empower jobhunters to make future career decisions based on their own individual preferences. The company aims to liberate jobhunters by helping them understand themselves and by understanding that life is self-determined and full of choices.

Jobsite treats jobhunters with respect, which is especially important in the recruitment industry, and communicates with them as equals. By showing its human side with company blogs, jobhunters can find out what's happening behind the scenes at Jobsite. Jobsite dedicates its days to helping jobhunters understand what they really want.

www.jobsite.co.uk

Not everyone wants to grab a sandwich at their desk.

Cramming in a super-chilled bloomer between phone calls isn't everyone's idea of a lunch-hour (more like a lunch ten minutes). Especially when you could be catching up with friends in the park.

If you're looking for a new job right now, or you're curious about what's out there, see www.jobsite.co.uk

Jobsite. Because different people want different things from their work life.

www.jobsite.co.uk

2000
– Jobsite launches the UK's first personalised candidate homepage: 'My Jobsite'.

2003
– Jobsite signs an international partnership with Careerbuilder.com.

2004
– Associated New Media (ANM), a division of Associated Newspapers Ltd (DMGT), the publishers of the Daily Mail, acquires Jobsite.

2004
– Jobsite establishes the European Recruitment Alliance (ERA) with leading online recruitment sites across Europe.

61

Littlewoods
even more

Market Context

Littlewoods even more is a department store in the home that gives consumers access to an array of fashion, footwear, home and leisure products. It is part of Littlewoods Shop Direct Home Shopping Limited, the largest home shopping (mail order) operator within the UK, with an annual turnover of £2.1 billion.

The UK has a long history of home shopping that, in recent years, has experienced rapid growth, driven mainly by online sales. 17% of Littlewoods Shop Direct Group's total turnover is currently generated through e-commerce, making it one of the UK's largest online non-food retailers.

Littlewoods even more has the biggest UK market share in home shopping, currently valued at £11.1 billion. Through its 'one-stop shop'

format, Littlewoods even more aims to remain the nation's first choice in home shopping by providing customers with the ability to purchase the lifestyle they desire – today.

As the brand name suggests Littlewoods even more offers high street prices with 'even more' –
free credit, free delivery, free returns and 10% cashback, should customers choose to subscribe.

Achievements

Through both its catalogue and website Littlewoods even more offers customers access to around 16,640 product lines and more than 40,000 products including fashion, home interiors, garden furniture and equipment, up-to-date electrical goods, gadgets, technology and travel accessories. The brand is currently the largest non-specialist sports retailer in the UK and the fifth biggest mobile phone retailer.

Its 1,500 delivery vehicles transport around 14.9 million parcels a year. Customers of Littlewoods even more rate it number one for speed of delivery and for locating items of interest online.

Products and Services

Littlewoods even more stocks dozens of well-known brands, ranging from fashion brands such as Miss Sixty and Diesel, to homeware and technology brands like Dorma, Sony and Kodak. It also has a value-for-money own brand range. Products are updated on a regular basis throughout the year, to keep consumers informed of the latest trends in homes and fashion.

Littlewoods even more offers consumers the choice of how, where and when to shop by providing the flexibility to order by phone until 11pm or to shop online 24 hours a day.

This convenience extends to its delivery service. As a remote retailer Littlewoods even more delivers (and collects returns) within 48 hours, free of charge. For a small charge customers can arrange a specific day for delivery that better suits their schedule.

Littlewoods even more offers customers a choice of payment methods to make purchases both affordable and convenient. For instance, they can choose to spread costs, interest free, over 20 or 52 weeks and some may also qualify for 'buy now pay later' with a payment

holiday of between 6-12 months. Customers can now shop, open accounts and check statements online; the site is constantly evolving with new features being added all the time to make it easier to shop with Littlewoods even more.

The 'even more Magazine', produced in conjunction with Condé Nast, includes a combination of lifestyle features and the latest fashion and homeware spreads to extend consumer choice. One million copies of the magazine are distributed nationwide.

Personality and Goals

Littlewoods even more is the convenient, affordable and secure choice for shopping online, offering a wide selection of top brands at competitive prices. Its brand values are synonymous with the Littlewoods name, offering accessible and affordable quality goods. It has a modern, straightforward approach that appeals to a range of customers who want to make choices to fit their lifestyle.

www.littlewoods.com

1999 – Website launches as a 'closed site' (customers only) offering an alternative method of ordering.

2000 – Product categories are introduced to enable customers to browse before ordering. 'My Account' launches to enable customers to manage accounts online.

2001 – Website opens to everyone with enhanced online shopping facilities.

2004 – Littlewoods even more launches.

2005 – Mark Newton-Jones becomes the new Chief Executive of the newly renamed Littlewoods Shop Direct Home Shopping Limited.

Market Context

Men's lifestyle magazines have been one of the biggest and most interesting sectors of the publishing industry for the last 10 years. The so-called 'lads mag' sector exploded in the mid to late 1990s, with titles such as Maxim, Loaded, FHM, Arena, Esquire and GQ seeing rocket-fuelled growth. The rise of Britpop, the booming popularity of football and a celebration of British 'laddism' all helped define a new publishing genre. More recently, that growth has slowed, with ABC, from August 2005, showing total circulation of monthly men's lifestyle magazines had declined 4% year-on-year. A new breed of weekly men's titles, such as Zoo and Nuts, have changed the dynamic of the market, with each seeing rapid growth.

As a sign of their greater maturity, leading monthly titles including Maxim have diversified, both by launching overseas versions, and also expanding into online and mobile media. The sector has also split into two groups: the mass-market titles FHM and Loaded, going for younger readers, and more upmarket titles with older readerships, such as Maxim, Arena, GQ and Esquire.

Maxim is leading the sector's diversification. It is now published in print in 43 countries, online in 10 countries and has a mobile presence in 22 countries. Online revenues increased by over 20% in 2005 and that growth is set to accelerate in 2006.

Achievements

Maxim magazine is the most successful men's magazine in the world and recently celebrated its 10th anniversary. In a challenging and rapidly changing publishing sector – which has seen many titles come and go over the last decade – Maxim has remained firm, successfully diversified outside of the UK and into new media.

www.maximmag.co.uk has received numerous high profile industry awards, including Best Cross Media Project in the AOP Online Publishing Awards 2005, Best Use of Multiple Channels in the New Media Age Effectiveness Awards 2004, and Best Designed Magazine on the Web in the 2000 Magazine Design Awards.

Products and Services

www.maximmag.co.uk has built its success on several key products. One of the best-known and most in-demand is Maxim Girls – a state-of-the-art online showcase for 10 years' worth of Maxim beauties, such as Beyoncé Knowles, Sienna Miller, Cameron Diaz, Paris

HISTORY

1995 – Maxim Magazine is launched in the UK by Dennis Publishing. A year earlier, IPC's Loaded had helped create the lads mag phenomenon – celebrating a culture of sex, booze, music and football.

1996 – Maxim Online launches as one of the showcase brands of Dennis Publishing's new online division, Dennis Interactive.

1997 – Maxim launches in the US.

1999 – By the end of the year, the 'big th men's monthlies, FHM, Loaded and Maxir account for about three-quarters of the mark by sales value (Source: MagForum.com).

Hilton, Billie Piper and Avril Lavigne. Maxim Girls comes complete with high resolution photos, interviews and downloads.

Another popular product is Maxim TV, providing exclusive, behind-the-scenes access to Maxim magazine's photoshoots, showing what goes into making women like Abi Titmuss and Paris Hilton look so glamorous.

Stupid Fun is a searchable archive of jokes, viral video clips, funnies and games

that readers can scatter around each other's email in-trays.

Tapping into the boom in mobile phone photography, the Our Gallery section allows readers to instantly send fun pictures directly from their mobiles to appear on the website.

And, meeting demand for online betting services, the site also has Maxim Bet – a comprehensive gambling portal with advice, videos, tips and player profiles for sports betting, casino betting and online poker.

For men on the look-out for love and fun, Maxim Date is a joint venture with Speeddater.co.uk which has a database of over 100,000 single girls.

Personality and Goals

The Maxim brand is aimed at smart men who appreciate women, good humour and all those other things that take the edges off life's sharp corners. If it was a person, Maxim would be the sort of bloke you'd love to chat to in a pub (as long as you're buying).

www.maximmag.co.uk

Market Context

In today's climate of fierce competition, the personal finance market has become increasingly complex and confusing to the consumer. Consumers are growing in sophistication when purchasing or switching personal finance products and will shop around, often online, to find the best deal. Moneynet aims to meet this need by providing a one-stop-shop that is fast and easy to use.

At Moneynet the goal is to make the process of finding the right mortgage, the best home for your savings or the best credit card or loan a simple one. Moneynet aims to achieve this by presenting financial data in an interactive, clear and easy to understand format.

Achievements

Launched in 1997, Moneynet was the first UK website to publish a comprehensive, independent and impartial overview of the products available in the personal finance sector, thus giving the consumer the freedom and ease to choose the product best suited to their needs. Moneynet offered consumers the first real alternative to brokers and traditional information sources in their search to compare and select personal finance products.

The company can be credited with originally devising the concept of an online personal finance product aggregation service. It set the model for the rest of the market to follow.

Today, Moneynet is frequently quoted in the financial press and regularly used by press, TV and radio as a reliable source for industry comment. Total visits to Moneynet reached more than 1.48 million in 2004, while unique visitors topped one million.

Products and Services

Moneynet's portfolio includes details of mortgage products from more than 100 lenders, investment products from over 100 banks and building societies, plus details of many more credit card and personal loan providers, all of which are updated daily.

Moneynet provides online comparison and application tools for personal loans, secured loans, credit cards, mortgages, life insurance, savings and deposit accounts, cash ISA's and general insurance. It also offers an account aggregation service, product guides, calculators and wizards. The Moneynet newsletter, Moneyfocus, is regularly sent to a registered database of over 90,000 users and contains exclusive industry comment from independent financial journalists, as well as product evaluation and consumer awareness guides.

Moneynet stands out in a crowded market by providing a trusted source of impartial and accurate information along with a clear and simple user interface.

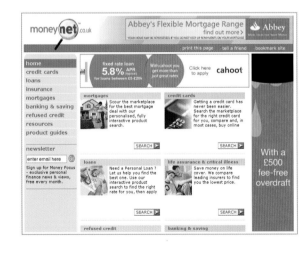

HISTORY

1997
– Moneynet launches as the UK's first online mortgage comparison site of its kind.

1998
– Credit cards and loans are added to the site to offer a more rounded personal finance site.

2000
– Moneynet raises institutional investment.

2001
– Moneynet's product range is extended to include insurance products.

THINGS YOU DIDN'T KNOW...

▌ More than £750 million worth of life insurance cover is requested via Moneynet each month.

▌ There are more than 6,000 products available to compare on the Moneynet site, all updated daily.

▌ More than 5,000 credit cards and in excess of 11,000 personal loans are applied for via Moneynet each month.

Personality and Goals

As a brand, Moneynet strives to be an impartial, trustworthy, friendly and easy-to-use consumer champion.

Moneynet exists to provide impartial, clear, jargon-free information to help visitors compare and decide upon the best products for their circumstances. Its goal is to help save the consumer money and reduce the time spent making purchasing decisions.

www.moneynet.co.uk

2002	2003	2004	2005
– Moneynet undergoes a brand re-design.	*– Moneynet launches its account aggregation service.*	*– Moneynet undergoes a site re-design to improve speed and usability.*	*– Moneynet launches a newsletter and product guides.*

Ⓜ MOONFRUIT™

Market Context

Moonfruit operates as a software provider within the European internet hosting market, estimated to be worth approximately 4 billion euros per year (Source: Forrester 2003). Of this, around 500 million euros is classified as shared hosting; domain name providers, shared hosting providers, and hosting software providers, like Moonfruit.

Shared hosting is growing at a rate of 18% per year (Source: Forrester 2003) – the fastest in the hosting domain. Although the software component of this market is one of the smallest and most fragmented sectors, it remains one of the fastest growing.

The European hosting market is currently experiencing a period of consolidation with its big players, 1&1, Pipex/Host Europe and Lycos Europe, acquiring smaller companies to provide a full range of shared services. In consensus with this general consolidation of the marketplace, Moonfruit, which stood out as a successful, independent, software provider, has recently been acquired to form part of a new European hosting group.

Achievements

Since the launch of moonfruit.com in January 2000 over 750,000 people have used SiteMaker to build and develop both business and individual websites (Moonfruit Internal Audit 2005). Moonfruit continues to record around 50 million monthly hits, over all of its sites, with some 18,000 new customers trying out the software each month.

It is an achievement in itself that Moonfruit survived the dotcom crash, which claimed many scalps within the industry, and have since turned the business into a commercial success, doubling sales each year for the last three.

This success owes much to the unique nature of Moonfruit's Flash based website building tool and the fact that it is the only major website builder using this technology.

Recognised for innovation through a host of design and interactive awards – winning BBC2's 'Best Online Design Award' in its inaugural year – Moonfruit's industry accolades, include 'Most Innovative Online Business' (Revolution March 2001) and 'Best Application Award' (Flash Film Festival 2005).

HISTORY

2000 – Moonfruit.com launches with a free product that includes investment by Bain & Company, Europatweb, and Macromedia.

2000 – Moonfruit launches SiteMaker 2.0, incorporating a new moonfruit.com design.

2001 – The first subscription product, Moonfruit SiteMaker 3.0, launches. Its new designs and logos create a brand separation between SiteMaker and moonfruit.com.

2002 – Moonfruit's management team buy up all company assets, to avoid bankruptcy during the dot.com crash.

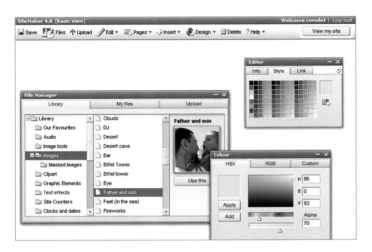

Products and Services

Moonfruit provides software that allows users, with no previous web technology experience, to build and develop websites. There is no requirement to learn any programming languages or specific web codes; users are limited only by their own imaginations.

The software features unique drag and drop tools to allow users to edit and introduce site items and facilities by clicking a mouse. Adaptations, like a message board, shopping basket or chat room, can be achieved through a simple click and drag format.

Users can either obtain the Moonfruit SiteMaker 4.0 software free – with advertising – or as a

subscription product. Subscriptions start at £2.99 per month for a fully customised website, through to £15.99 per month for a top-of-the-range pack, with ecommerce features, group mailing lists and additional extras.

Personality and Goals

The Moonfruit brand is quirky, friendly, and approachable. Website building, particularly for the inexperienced, can be daunting. Moonfruit strives to overcome this by creating a sense of community: encouraging customers to interact and support each other via a vibrant online forum. By breaking down technological barriers, Moonfruit enables any user to build a high quality website simply and quickly.

The brand inspires loyalty, creates connections and encourages a sense of shared ownership. Many customers grow with Moonfruit, continuing to support its development and other interactive users.

www.moonfruit.com

2003 – A period of steady growth and consolidation ensues, during which time Joe White returns as Moonfruit managing director.

2004 – Moonfruit SiteMaker 4.0 launches, with a distribution deal agreed with Lycos Europe.

2004 – Moonfruit signs a contract with Channel 4 to use SiteMaker as part of its Origination Project – putting British culture firmly online.

2005 – Moonfruit SiteMakerFree launches in July, heralding the return of a free product.

2005 – Moonfruit is acquired as part of a new European hosting group.

Achievements

MyTravel.com was launched in November 2000 and the site recently made its millionth sale. Every week over 10,000 people travel on an online booking made through MyTravel.

Internet bookings across MyTravel's UK websites have increased by over 70%, year-on-year, with the average selling price per holiday up by one-fifth and now accounting for over 15% of MyTravel's total UK business as opposed to just 8.5% a year ago.

In May 2005, Hitwise named MyTravel as the fifth most popular travel website, a commendable achievement considering the company's 'word of mouth' promotional strategy. Combined MyTravel sites now receive on average 1.25 million unique monthly visitors.

Products and Services

MyTravel.com is the only place where customers can find the group's full range of products. With a portfolio that covers holidays, flights,

Market Context

Holidays were one of the first major purchases made by the public online and it is significant that, even today, 54% of all UK internet searches are travel-related – the European average is 48%. Although recent world events have affected the holiday market, the British public's enthusiasm for booking travel online (coupled with a huge increase in broadband subscriptions) has seen a market rise in total online spending of 60% over the past two years.

In 2004, UK consumers took approximately 19 million package holidays, spending a total of £13 billion on travel. MyTravel.com is the main consumer website for the MyTravel Group which incorporates, among other brands, Airtours, Aspro, Going Places, Direct Holidays, Hotelstogo, Manos, Cresta and Late Escapes. It is also one of the UK's 'big four' tour operators alongside Thomas Cook, First Choice and Thomson.

The statistics show that the British public is comfortable with booking travel-related products online and MyTravel.com offers a technologically advanced system, leading holiday guides and product range to satisfy the old adage 'something for everyone'.

HISTORY

1999 – *Direct Holidays branded website launches as a precursor to MyTravel.com and becomes the first fully transactional holiday site in the UK.*

2000 – *MyTravel.com website launches. Within two months Hitwise reports that it has gained 9% of the online travel market – a figure that outstrips both lastminute.com and Expedia.*

2001 – *The Late Escapes holiday auction site launches. Its 'Holidays From £1' auctions are the first of its kind in the UK.*

cruises, hotels, car hire, travel insurance, foreign currency and even theme park tickets, the website and supporting customer retention management activities are designed to enable customers to pick up everything they need prior to travel.

One of the site's powerful new developments – invisible to customers – is a cutting edge tracking system that monitors visitor usage and behavioural patterns. This helps experts to make informed judgments, from the first point of contact through to sales, and enables MyTravel to react quickly to changes in user behaviour. It also benefits customers by allowing them to locate products quickly and simply.

The accurate analysis of customer usage patterns is a major strategy achievement that began in January 2005 and was carried out in association with a specialist third party agency. MyTravel.com recognises the role of specialist third parties in a technologically complicated environment and in the last year alone has enjoyed successful relationships with keyword advertising, search engine optimisation and affiliated partnership agencies.

The information gleaned from these relationships, in tandem with the close relationship with MyTravel.com customers, has led to a number of site usability and functionality changes due for implementation in 2006. Other planned developments include one-way flight sales and the re-introduction of city break holidays.

Personality and Goals

MyTravel.com is a customer-focused brand with an emphasis on continual research and development. It strives to make the customer experience as enjoyable as possible and prides itself on a customer-facing interface that quickly delivers exactly what users are searching for; and having built up a loyal customer base through repeat users, it is clearly a successful strategy.

Its personality is responsive, creative and fun to reflect the notion that finding and booking holidays – for many users their major leisure purchase each year – should be just that: fun.

www.MyTravel.com

2001-2002 – *During a difficult period for the travel industry as a whole, MyTravel.com undergoes a major re-focusing and re-evaluation, significantly streamlining its products and online services.*

2004 – *A site overhaul implements a robust technology platform to allow more flexible and rapid responses to new opportunities.*

2005 – *The Digital Marketing Centre Of Excellence is formed – an in-house specialist team to guide the group's tour operators and specialist businesses, which in turn will advise and drive online strategies.*

myvillage.com

Market Context

There is little doubt that the online leisure market is big business; with many people now using the internet as a tool for researching pubs, bars, restaurants and clubs.

MyVillage identified a gap in the digital market for lively and slightly eccentric websites that detailed what was happening in local areas and turned the brand into the largest listings, events and features-led network of websites in the UK.

Users predominately fall into the category of young 25-40 year-old professionals, of which 68% are female and 32% male. Demographics show them to be affluent (earning upwards of £22,000 per annum, much of it disposable), media literate, trend-savvy and city and area proud. Mindful of its core users, MyVillage delivers a comprehensive service that covers customer's base needs and wants – with a few desires thrown in for good measure.

Main market competitors, for sites providing up-to-the-minute non-subscribed listings and feature information, are bbc.co.uk, ViewLondon and Itchy Guides.

Achievements

From modest beginnings MyVillage.com has grown into a dynamic network of 52 websites with over 600,000 unique monthly users.

Its ever-expanding team of far-flung writers and editors – each dedicated to finding the best and quirkiest event an area has to offer – interview the famous, and not so famous, in order to provide users with the latest information and gossip.

As a leading website for the Notting Hill Carnival, MyVillage is regularly called upon to comment on the annual carnival debate, in addition to hosting local star-studded award ceremonies that celebrate the best of each diverse area. Recipients of past awards include, DJ Norman Jay OBE, designer, Oswald Boateng and actress Leslie Ash.

By changing the content daily and through continually updating features, MyVillage has forged ahead of market rivals such as UpMyStreet and since its inception has seen a steady period of growth, supported by user appreciation and Google statistics.

Products and Services

MyVillage.com began as a hobby for Roifield Brown, who initially built a community website for his local area, Notting Hill. Under its first name of Portowebbo it caught the imagination of local West London 'Hillites'. The potential, of building a network of local listings and feature led websites, was recognised by Adam Cole (MyVillage

HISTORY

1999 – Roifield Brown launches a website called portowebbo – traffic on day one tops at five users.

2000 – Adam Cole becomes a partner in MyVillage and portowebbo changes to mynottinghill.co.uk.

2000 – Two more websites join the MyVillage network: MyChelsea and MyKensington.

2001 – MyVillage hosts the MyNottingHill awards for the best shop, bar and restaurant – the event gets media mentions in the Mirror, BBC, Sky TV and Hello magazine.

Chairman) and a collaboration between the two men led to MyVillage.com. The site works on the premise that every borough in London and every city in the UK should have its own local website – each unique while retaining the special MyVillage look and feel.

MyVillage has remained true to its original ideals, offering an enterprising brand that constantly updates news and opinion, gives user reviews and up-to-the-minute entertainment listings and provides a flexible forum for local knowledge.

MyVillage has its own distinct loyalty scheme, Passport, a privilege card offering members discounts and exclusive deals in some of the top shops, bars and clubs, within a specified area. Long-standing affiliations and partnerships have created a MyVillage 'one-stop shop' with top channels of Arts & Entertainment, Bars & Music, and Restaurants as well as Celebrity Photos. Present partners include: the Press Association, BigPictures, Clickajob, Flatmateclick, Dating channels and Restaurant Bookings.

Personality and Goals

MyVillage lives up to its ethos as a brand 'by the people for the people'. Its individualistic personality is delivered with a slice of style and an eye

for the quirkier side of life. It goes against the mainstream approach by backing up articles and features with an irrelevant sense of humour.

MyVillage plans for the future include, exporting the brand to every postcode in the UK and expanding its successful loyalty scheme, 'Passport'.

www.MyVillage.com

2001 – Inner London websites are added to the MyVillage network.

2003 – UK city websites are created as part of the MyVillage network.

2004 – Passport local loyalty card scheme launches, starting in Notting Hill and rolling out across London.

2005 – Traffic reaches 500,000 users, with three million pages impressions a month.

Market Context

Loyalty Management UK (LMUK) operates the UK Nectar Loyalty Programme. LMUK also owns Loyalty Management International, the company responsible for launching market leading multi-company loyalty programmes in the Netherlands, Spain, the United Arab Emirates and Canada – where more than 70% of households participate.

Nectar's website receives more than one million visits per month and is one of the UK's top 20 retail sites by reach (Source: Nielsen//NetRatings NetView UK February and September 2005).

In October 2005, LMUK launched Nectar eStores – a shopping portal accessed through www.nectar.com, offering Nectar points for purchases from over 70 online retailers.

This online extension of the Nectar brand further broadens the appeal of the UK's biggest loyalty programme to the millions of consumers who increasingly shop online.

Achievements

Over 50% of UK households participate in Nectar, the largest loyalty programme in the UK. It is the only true coalition loyalty programme to operate in the UK: 16 companies (known as sponsors) participate in Nectar to issue Nectar points to their customers – customers (collectors) earn more points, more quickly, using just one card.

An average collector shopping at all Nectar sponsors could earn points on 40% of their annual household expenditure; there are around 6,000 retail outlets where the Nectar card can be used to earn points. Incredibly, on average 19 Nectar cards are swiped every second of every day.

Furthermore, redemption of points is truly enormous: seven out of ten Nectar collectors have redeemed their points for rewards worth over £500 million in the first three years of Nectar's operation. Over 60% of 'Nectar to Your Door' – merchandise rewards – are redeemed online.

The current website was launched in February 2004 and is continually being enhanced. It was designed with collectors at its heart, a strategy that has proved very successful: user volumes have quadrupled, contact centre volumes have decreased significantly and consistently high customer satisfaction scores are being recorded. In September 2005, www.nectar.com was rated among the top 100 of all websites in the UK by reach (Source: Nielsen//NetRatings NetView UK).

In 2004, www.nectar.com was named winner of the British Interactive Media Association Awards – Retail Category.

rewards are sweeter at
www.nectar.com

HISTORY

2002 – *The Nectar programme launches with four sponsors and the original Nectar website. A massive launch campaign is undertaken across the UK on TV, radio, press, outdoor and in-store with its launch retail sponsors.*

2004 – *The new Nectar website – www.nectar.com – has been one year in the making and is designed with collectors at its heart.*

Products and Services

The Nectar website provides customers with an inexpensive and accessible way of keeping up-to-date with sponsor news, bonus points offers, and the latest Nectar developments. Once registered, which can be done completely online, collectors can update their account details, view statements and search through the whole range of rewards, many of which are redeemable online. The offline 'Rewards Catalogue' has been translated into an interactive and fully animated online experience.

An 'earn calculator' forecasts the time it will take a collector to earn their target reward based upon current spend. There is also an online store locator, embedding MultiMap's technology.

Emails are used extensively to support the Nectar programme, encompassing Nectar announcements, sponsor offers, rewards promotions, and points statements. Over 60 million personalised emails, across over 100 campaigns, were sent in the year to September 2005.

In early 2005, an opportunity was identified to expand the Nectar programme by developing an online shopping portal 'Nectar eStores' within www.nectar.com, where collectors could earn points for purchasing from leading online retailers.

Retailers are grouped into multiple categories and collectors can browse Nectar eStores like a virtual shopping centre. Over 500,000 products are indexed and a collector can use the powerful search facility to find products by price, keywords, category and retailer.

Personality and Goals

The core of Nectar's brand essence is 'Better off Together'. The brand values are built around working in partnership, being easy to understand and rewarding customer loyalty. They, along with the brand's engaging, responsive and innovative personality, have directly contributed to Nectar's popularity and success.

www.nectar.com

NetNames^{NN}

Market Context

NetNames is a specialist provider of corporate domain name management services. It provides a full, outsourced service for the registration, renewal and management of domain name portfolios.

There are around 80 million domain names registered worldwide and this is growing each quarter. Growth is being driven by factors such as the introduction of new domain name suffixes, the use of unique domain names for the marketing of products and services and the interest in local market suffixes or country-code top-level domain names (ccTLDs). A major new suffix on the horizon is the new .eu domain, which will become available in 2006.

The potential market for domain name management services is large. It applies to any business with a serious interest in protecting and maintaining its brand on the internet. At the very least, this includes all of the FTSE 350 in the UK, the Fortune 1000 in the US and all other multi-nationals and major brand owners around the world. In fact, Platinum Service is available to any company with more than 50 domain names and, with research showing that companies own 75% of the 80 million domain names worldwide; the potential market is clearly vast.

Achievements

Set up in the UK more than 10 years ago, NetNames is the UK market leader in domain name management services, with more than 30 of the FTSE 100 companies signed up to its prestigious Platinum Service. Its customers include many of the world's leading companies and brand owners. For three consecutive years, NetNames has been named in the Deloitte & Touche Technology Fast 50.

Products and Services

The need for companies to manage their brands on the internet is now of vital importance. NetNames has more than ten years' experience in the domain name industry and works with many of the world's major corporations.

Who's looking out for you on the Internet?

NetNames Platinum Service – Corporate Domain Name Management

It isn't easy managing and protecting your identity on the Internet. One thing's for sure, cybersquatters, competitors and rapidly changing markets aren't making it any easier. That's why leading companies, including over 30% of the FTSE 100, have turned to NetNames Platinum Service to effectively manage and protect their domain names around the world.

NetNames takes the complexity and risk out of domain name management. Whether it's helping you formulate your global domain name strategy, ongoing monitoring and management of your portfolio or recovery of lost domains, we'll ensure you cover all of your bases, all of the time.

Key features of Platinum Service include:

- Guaranteed domain renewal
- Dedicated account management
- NetNames Portfolio Manager
- Simple and flexible invoicing
- Global domain name coverage

Time to choose a partner who'll look out for you? Time to choose NetNames.

UK/Europe: +44 (0)870 458 9401
USA: +1 212 627 4599
platinum@netnames.com

www.netnames.com

NetNames^{NN}

HISTORY

1995
– NetNames launches in the UK.

1999
– NetNames orchestrates international expansion into the US and continental Europe.

1999
– NetNames becomes an ICANN Accredited Registrar.

2002
– NetNames Platinum Service launches, and the company is recognised by Deloitte & Touche as Technology Fast 50 Winner.

Independent research has shown **NetNames** to be one of the world's most recognised domain name services companies.

More than 50% of TV ads now contain a domain name. This includes a growing trend to use campaign-specific URLs (known as **CURLS**) such as Norwich Union's quotemehappy.com and Renault's vavavoom.co.uk.

After .com, .de (Germany) is the second most popular domain name.

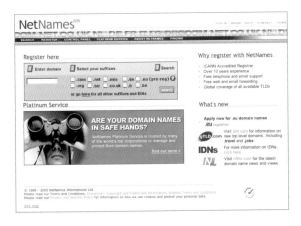

NetNames Platinum Service is a unique solution designed to help corporations and Intellectual Property (IP) professionals establish, implement and maintain an effective domain name management strategy.

The service is designed to provide peace of mind and delivers benefits such as: guaranteed domain renewal, dedicated account management, NetNames Portfolio Manager (online software application), simple and flexible invoicing and global domain name coverage.

All Platinum Service clients receive a dedicated account manager who provides advice and assists with the ongoing management of clients' domain names. On a day-to-day basis, the account manager takes responsibility for as much of the administration as the client requires. This can include managing transfers, consolidating portfolios and making technical changes. This account manager approach means that clients have one single point of contact for all their domain name requirements.

More than 30 FTSE 100 companies, including British Airways, Royal Bank of Scotland, Hilton Group, William Hill and Reckitt Benckiser are now using NetNames Platinum Service.

Personality and Goals

NetNames is focused on the corporate market. It aims to provide a high quality service, which means striving for professionalism in everything it does, from its systems to its people. The NetNames Platinum Service is founded on the belief that domain names are highly valuable company assets that need to be treated with the same level of importance as trademarks and offline brands.

www.netnames.com

2003

– More than 200 customers are using the Platinum Service, including many of the world's leading corporations and brands.

2004

– More than 400 customers, including 30 of the FTSE 100 companies, are now using NetNames Platinum Service. The company is again recognised in Deloitte's Technology Fast 50.

Market Context

Law firm websites are rarely popular. They invariably have names that match those of the firm behind them; they are seldom updated with fresh content – because lawyers are too busy; they contain confusing terminology; and when targeting technology companies, law firms' marketing materials tend to display clichéd images of circuit boards or headlines with terrible puns.

OUT-LAW.COM is part of Pinsent Masons, a firm that ranks in the top 15 law firms in the UK. The website focuses on IT and e-commerce legal issues but avoids these common pitfalls. The name was chosen to appeal to dynamic companies in a way that traditionally 'stuffy' law firm names do not. The sheriff's badge logo was designed by James Cameron of Laveron to reflect the innovative nature of the firm. Content is updated daily by an experienced full-time editorial team. Whereas most firms will claim to communicate with clients in plain English, with OUT-LAW, Pinsent Masons substantiate this claim by applying good journalism to explain complex issues, without the legalese.

This has helped to make OUT-LAW.COM one of the most popular law firm websites in the world, with almost 30,000 registered users and over twice that number visiting the site monthly. OUT-LAW Magazine – a hard copy publication to complement the online service – is read regularly by more than 27,000 people.

In comparison to mainstream consumer sites these figures may seem small; but for a law firm they are unparalleled.

Achievements

As the only law firm with e-Superbrand status, Pinsent Masons has a legitimate claim to being a leading online legal brand in the UK. The brand started off as it intended to continue when it was named 'Best Legal Website' in its inaugural year at the Legal IT

Awards in 2000. Since then it has won a host of other national and international awards, including the Market Disruptor Award at the US College of Law Practice Management's InnovAction Awards in Chicago in 2004.

Products and Services

OUT-LAW provides a service for organisations requiring help with IT and e-commerce legal issues. It also offers a full range of legal services, such as corporate and employment advice, to technology companies.

 HISTORY

2000
– Masons launches OUT-LAW.COM.

2001 – OUT-LAW Magazine launches, a hard copy spin-off of the website that is published three times a year and provides a range of articles and opinion pieces not featured on the website.

2001 – First series of OUT-LAW Breakfast Seminars are launched.

2002 – OUT-LAW News starts appearing in Google News, a first for any law firm.

Typical OUT-LAW.COM users include IT directors, entrepreneurs, human resource managers, data protection officers, in-house lawyers, software firms, retailers, banks and public authorities.

The site provides more than 6,000 pages of free legal information that includes legal news and guides on issues such as selling online, data protection and intellectual property. Sample contracts and checklists are also available to help both start-ups and established businesses.

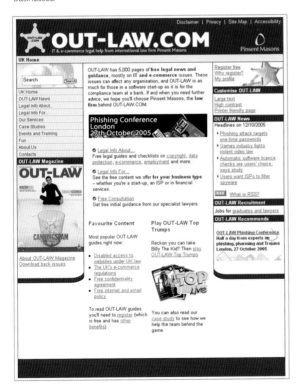

Another popular service is OUT-LAW Compliance which, for a fixed fee, provides a legal review of any website to assist compliance with UK laws.

Personality and Goals

OUT-LAW provides invaluable help and understanding in the field of IT and e-commerce law in a clear and concise way, devoid of legal jargon. Its brand values are innovative and ambitious, reflecting those of Pinsent Masons, with an aim to sustain its edge as a leading online legal brand. Its reputation for first-rate legal journalism fits in with its creative, humorous and modern personality that seeks to challenge the outdated notion of staid, old-fashioned law firms.

www.OUT-LAW.COM

THINGS YOU DIDN'T KNOW...

Rival law firms often direct their staff to **OUT-LAW.COM** as the best way to keep up-to-date with **IT law** – as many as 35 lawyers at a single rival firm are registered with the website.

Unusually for a legal website, **OUT-LAW.COM** offers users the opportunity to play games online. One of the most popular is an **OUT-LAW** branded version of Top Trumps that features western gunfighters.

2003 – *OUT-LAW In-House launches – allowing in-house legal teams to supplement their own resources or permitting those with no in-house team to benefit from a wide range of legal skills for a set monthly fee.*

2004 – *OUT-LAW Compliance launches.*

2004 – *Masons merges with Pinsents to become Pinsent Masons.*

2005 – *Pinsent Masons launches the latest version of OUT-LAW.COM.*

PhotoBox™

Market Context

The digital photography market has undergone incredible growth in the past five years. Market growth can be attributed to the increase of consumer broadband penetration, speed, and falling prices. In 2004, an estimated total of 2,111 million digital images were captured in the UK – of these, 260 million were printed at home, 174 million were photofinished, and of these, 66 million digital images (38%) were printed online (Source: Understanding and Solutions 2004).

The UK online photofinishing industry was worth £24 million in 2004 and is forecast to double by 2007 (Source: Understanding and Solutions 2004). This growth in mass-market online photo processing is fuelled by increasing competition – prices compare favourably to high street and home printing, with standard 6" x 4" prints available online from 7p each.

As an online digital photo service providing customers with efficient, affordable, and imaginative ways to print, store, and share their digital photos, PhotoBox has embraced this shift in the photographic market.

Achievements

Using award-winning, state-of-the-art facilities, and partnering with Fujifilm UK, PhotoBox has become a destination site for professional and amateur digital photographers, and now any new digital camera owner.

PhotoBox has amassed many accolades since its launch in June 2000. Most recently, it was named as the winner of the Choice Award by What Digital Camera magazine, and was listed as one of the '100 sites you can't live without' by the Daily Express.

In 2004 PhotoBox launched white label photo services for clients including Tiscali, This is Travel, Woolworths, NTL, Virgin.net, and Carphone Warehouse, whose new camera phones sold include a free PhotoBox trial.

Products and Services

PhotoBox customers can order photographic prints in an extensive range of sizes and gifts. Prints from passport prints, and standard 6" x 4" size up to 30" x 20" posters are available, while the gift range includes stretched canvas prints, mugs, T-shirts, make-up bags, beach bags, key rings, coasters, placemats, cushions, calendars, and much more. Many of the products are unique to the web. Standard-size prints ordered before 4pm Monday-Friday are dispatched the same day by first class post.

PhotoBox continuously strives to add new gifts and inventive ways for its customers to have fun with their photos. Free eCards were launched in August 2005, while October 2005 saw the launch of PhotoBox's PhotoBook – a coffee table album that features customers' chosen photos, photo captions, and a choice of page designs.

HISTORY

2000 – PhotoBox is founded by Graham Hobson (CEO) and Mark Chapman (MD).

2001 – PhotoBox provides a print ordering service for the second Big Brother TV series.

2002 – PhotoBox launches white label photo services for clients including Telewest Blueyonder, Internet Cameras Direct and Wanadoo.

2002 – PhotoBox launches PrintButton (www.printbutton.com), enabling e-commerce, print and gift ordering, and fulfilment for imaging websites, image archives and libraries.

PhotoBox also offers a number of mobile features for customers on the move. Its website is camera phone friendly, so that customers can upload photos from their phone into their free album space, send postcards from their mobile, and send their favourite pictures to any mobile for free.

Personality and Goals

PhotoBox's main purpose has always been to offer an excellent online experience, great quality products, and outstanding customer service. PhotoBox is customer-focused, with a fully trained in-house customer services team that listens to feedback and offers knowledgeable advice.

Quality and turnaround is controlled by producing all prints and almost all gifts in-house on the company's own machines. PhotoBox operates a no-quibble refund and re-do policy.

Uploading, storing, and sharing photos is free – PhotoBox customers are happy to share their photos with friends and family. Last time PhotoBox asked, 98% of customers rated the service as good or excellent, and just under 100% of customers said they would recommend PhotoBox to other people.

www.photobox.co.uk

Picture by member Joshua Atticks | Handstand | Newgale beach, Wales *[submit photo]*

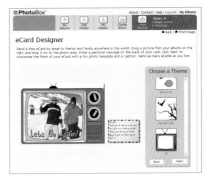

2003 – PhotoBox ...ate of the art laboratory ...nd larger HQ opens in ...rk Royal, London.

2004 – PhotoBox's free professional gallery (www.photoboxgallery.com) service launches. Pro Gallery enables professional photographers to create their own microsite that can be used to showcase and sell images online.

2004 – The re-designed PhotoBox website launches and features members own photos on the frontpage.

2005 – PhotoBox celebrates its fifth birthday and commissions a new high-capacity production facility with a three fold increase in production capacity.

81

Market Context

With internet penetration now at more than 60% of the population, and 53% of these connecting via broadband (Source: NOP/IUPS December 2004), the net has become part of the fabric of life. Indeed, property websites have grown massively in popularity over the past few years, with 89% of people looking to move house now searching online for appropriate properties (Source: Estate Agency News).

The UK residential property market remains huge with just under a million transactions in the year to March 2005 (Source: Land Registry). To ease the search process for house-hunters and estate agents, it is now commonplace for estate agents to run their own websites and to be part of one or more property search portals.

In 2000, more than 130 property-related websites existed. By 2005 the portals market had consolidated dramatically. Today, Primelocation's most serious competitors are Rightmove and Findaproperty, though these are strongest in the volume sector.

Launched in 2001, Primelocation.com is a leading UK search portal for prime property for sale and to let. The business was set up and funded by a group of more than 200 estate agents, led by Savills and Knight Frank, which saw the opportunity to create a definitive and exclusive property website.

Achievements

Primelocation launched in 2001 with 700 offices and 28,000 properties from 200 leading agent investors. Today it lists more than 200,000 UK and international properties from 3,500 agent offices.

More than a million people visit Primelocation.com monthly, and about 50% of these are return visitors. These visitors conduct some two million property searches and more than five million full property details pages are viewed.

With its exclusive listings policy, whereby Primelocation's agents commit not to feature their properties on any other property portal, it effectively dominates the online segment of properties for sale over £500,000. Around 80% of properties advertised in Country Life or The London Magazine are to be found on Primelocation.com and on no competitor property portal.

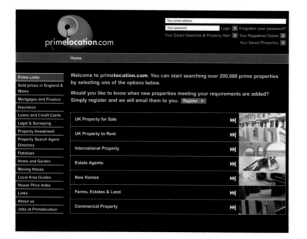

 Primelocation's on TV this Autumn. Don't miss out.

To join (or re-join), just call Mark Foley or Stewart Black on **020 7432 4000** or e-mail **agentenquiries@primelocation.com**.

HISTORY **2001** – *Primelocation.com launches as a UK search portal for prime property for sale and to let.*

September 2003 – *Primelocation Magazine launches in central London as a way of gaining major visibility and brand awareness on the back of traditional agent offline advertising.*

Products and Services

Primelocation.com allows consumers to specify the kind of property they are looking for and to get further information about all the site's properties that match their criteria, then to contact the agent who is handling the property. Consumers can specify the location, the type of property, the budget (minimum or maximum) and the required number of bedrooms. They can even provide key-words (stables, swimming pool, etc.) to pin down the property selection. Users can register to receive e-mail alerts as soon as new, appropriate properties become available.

In addition to searching, users can also access information to get the most out of their move or to make the most of their current property. This includes sold property prices, information about mortgages, details of moving services providers, directories of home improvement providers and local area guides.

Personality and Goals

Much of the brand's personality is encapsulated in the word 'prime'. It aims to convey, through the brand's tone of voice and graphic design, the excellence of the business: the quality of member agents, their properties, partners, management team and so forth. The word 'prime' is an estate agent's textbook way of describing high quality, especially in the context of 'location, location, location'.

Primelocation's goal is to become the ultimate property website, positioned and perceived as the definitive one-stop-shop for effective property searching, selling and letting.

www.primelocation.com

RIVER ISLAND

www.riverisland.com

Market Context

With the womenswear outerwear & footwear market valued at just over £13.4 billion (a growth of 3% year-on-year) and menswear estimated at £8.2 billion (static year-on-year), River Island operates in a highly competitive and fragmented environment (Source: TNS Fashion Trak 52 w/e July 24th 2005). Consumers are becoming more and more demanding for faster fashion at better value, which is reflected in response times on the high street with products being turned around faster than ever at even lower prices. The high street multiples such as Topshop/Topman, New Look, Next, Dorothy Perkins and Burtons all compete aggressively for market share with product being key to entice consumers in store – the faster they can turn the latest trends around, and deliver it with the best value, the better.

More recently supermarkets and discounters entered the market place and are stealing share away from middle market retailers. This has led to the market becoming more polarised with the value-discount retailers at one end of the scale and added value retailers at the other.

The web marketplace is a fast moving market, with many key 'bricks and mortar' retailers having transactional websites to compete with pure online retailers. Key players competing with www.riverisland.com are the likes of ASOS, Topshop/Topman, Miss Selfridge and Warehouse, with other retailers such as H&M, Oasis and New Look having pure brand and information based sites.

The UK market and the consumer River Island targets is becoming increasingly web savvy with 63% of households having used the internet (86% of 15-19 year olds and 79% of 20-24 year olds) and 39% actually shopping online (44% of 15-24 years olds – 14% spending on clothing) – (Source: TGI Jan-Dec 2004).

Achievements

Over the past two years, River Island has been increasing market share steadily showing a 48% increase in share within the women's target audience and a 26% increase in the men's (Source: TNS Fashion Track w/e April 3rd 2005 (Target audience 16-39 yrs) merged with River Island sales figures).

RIVER ISLAND

HISTORY

Mid 1950s – River Island begins trading under the name Lewis Separates.

Late 1960s – The brand goes through several name changes, most recognisably becoming Chelsea Girl in 1967.

Mid 1970s – The brand sets up its first in-house design team creating its own bespoke style and look.

Late 1980s – The name River Island is first used. The original wooden floored, East Coast inspired shop design is unveiled.

www.riverisland.com boasts well over 100,000 visitors per week, with a peak of over 150,000 (June 2005), which places it in the top 10 of online fashion retailers (based on market share).

Recent industry and customer recognition awards include the Drapers Record Multiple Retailer or the Year 2004; Retail Week 7th Annual Retail Interior Awards; Fashion Interior of the Year; More Fashion Awards 2004; Retailer of the Year, More Fashion Awards 2004; Most Aspirational Mail Order Catalogue, Company High Street Awards 2004; Most improved shop on the High Street, Company High Street Awards 2005; Best bags, as well as the FHM 100 Doors 2004 – finalist.

With the brand in such a strong position, River Island recently developed an awareness campaign to announce those strengths to the target audience. The advertising campaign is about to enter its second year and comprises single and double page spreads shot using models the River Island customer is able to associate with. By working closely with its customers, River Island knows that the campaign is delivering the standard of material that they have come to expect from the River Island brand, relating directly to them and their own individual lifestyles. Early indications of spontaneous brand awareness are already showing signs of improvement.

Products and Services

The internet is the ideal medium for a brand like River Island in that it is constantly changing and evolving; instantly. Just as in River Island's stores nationwide where customers come back regularly and expect

to see change. The team has developed processes to allow new product to arrive online every day, just as product comes off display as soon as it starts to break down. Basically it's like a flagship online.

River Island womenswear is committed to selling individual clothes for individual people. They are youthful, confident, stylish and fun. Menswear on the other hand is about providing cool clothes for men who want to look good and feel great without trying too hard.

River Island offers a complete wardrobe solution enabling it to continue to grow its share of wallet across the market place through several types of market extension, from shoes to jewels.

Personality and Goals

River Island has two personalities. For the River Island girl, it's Successful, Classy, Sexy, Fun and Funky whilst confident and fashionable. River Island menswear is Confident, Contemporary, Authentic, Relaxed, Independent and Light hearted.

River Island has undergone an aggressive re-fit roll out strategy over the past year to support its strategy of being the 'best' on every high street; another example of constant refreshment and improvement. Regional flagship stores that represent this look include Manchester Trafford, Thurrock, Cardiff and Dublin Grafton Street as well as smaller stores such as Windsor. The Oxford Circus store has been open less than two years and has already had two 'updates'.

www.riverisland.com

Late 1990s
– River Island launches a website holding information about the brand.

2001
– RiverIsland.com launches as a fully transactional site.

Present day – The design led ethos of the business enables River Island to offer an innovative shopping experience in 200 outlets across eight countries, including its most recent in Dubai. A team of 60 designers are now employed to keep the collection at the forefront of fashion.

Market Context

In February 2005, 59% of adults in Great Britain had used the internet in the previous three months (Source: Office of National Statistics April 2005). Streetmap provides online map and location-based services to both the public and businesses. Users are able to search by postcode, place name, street name, telephone code, latitude and longitude, or grid reference.

Achievements

Streetmap is a leading UK provider of online maps supplied free to the public as well as location-based services to businesses. Streetmap is recognised as one of the dominant players within this marketplace. According to the Alexa directory, the largest human-edited directory on the web, Streetmap is the most popular UK mapping website.

Products and Services

Streetmap's services encompass both its public website, offering fast street-level maps for the whole of the UK, and its business service, which provides street-level maps of Europe, global atlas maps and 'find my nearest' services. The geographic map data is provided by Bartholomew and Ordnance Survey.

Streetmap's public website sticks to its brand ethos of 'quick and efficient'. Using the search box on the homepage, it normally takes just one click to navigate from the homepage to displaying a map. The site can be searched automatically by a variety of data, including postcode, street name or place name.

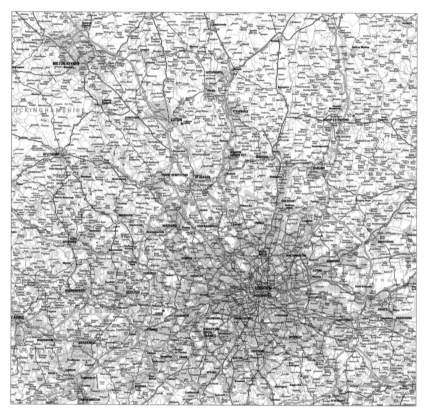

Streetmap's business services employ its powerful engine to help business users websites provide the now expected features of 'find-my-nearest' and location mapping.

Streetmap's 'find-my-nearest' service is a simple, fast, efficient service that can be integrated into a company's own web infrastructure. It provides searching not just by location, but by categories, attributes

HISTORY

1997 – *Streetmap started out with the simple concept of showing a London street level map with a quick-indexing look-up facility.*

1998 – *Streetmap became the first mapping provider to supply location based services to businesses across the UK.*

and ranges. Results can be filtered, weighted and randomised. The 'find-my-nearest' service can be used for a wide variety of uses, e.g. 'find my nearest store that delivers to me' might be used by a retail outlet, or 'find my nearest bus stop' may be used by a local services website or 'find properties in my area' may be used by an estate agent.

Streetmap's map service provides a 'quick map' system, integrated within the web page, which can show multiple levels of zoom, icons and navigation facilities.

Personality and Goals

Even in the borderless world of the internet, location is an important element that links users to the real world. Streetmap's goal is to provide location-based services to both the consumer and the business, which make that link simple, quick and efficient.

Streetmap's future plans include adding routing directions to both its public and business services, extending the visual presentation of its

maps, a new business-specific website at www.streetmap.biz and a new global service for the public at www.streetmap.com.

www.streetmap.co.uk

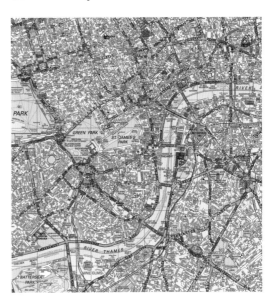

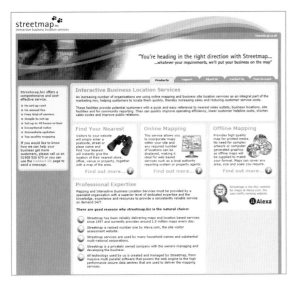

2000 – Streetmap develops its own in house sales team to sell advertising on the public website. The marketing of both these services was successful and ensured the profitability of Streetmap and also enabled the company to remain in private ownership, without the requirement for outside investment.

2005 – Still with its original team, Streetmap has become one of the most recognised internet brands, with a worldwide reputation for providing quality mapping services to millions of public users and numerous businesses.

TELETEXTHOLIDAYS.CO.UK

Market Context

With over 39.5 million overseas holidays taken by Britons in the last year and the constant proliferation of travel websites, Teletext Holidays continues to be a dominant force in the UK holiday market – not only via its TV origins but also online through its website www.teletextholidays.co.uk.

The strength of the Teletext brand name, coupled with significant marketing spends over the past few years, has made teletextholidays.co.uk one of UK consumers' favourite online travel sites. With 3.4 million unique users per month it recently took its place in the top five UK travel websites (Source: Hitwise 2005). The high volume of monthly users ensures maximum exposure for onsite advertisers.

As the number of holidays taken each year increases, teletextholidays.co.uk is poised to maintain its position as one of the UK's most used travel websites.

Achievements

Unlike many holiday websites, that attract a niche audience, teletextholidays.co.uk has retained its mass appeal. The site's audience represents a much wider geographical and socio-economic cross-section of society than other travel websites with people of all ages, ranging from 18 year-olds to over-55s, making up its core user group.

However, by understanding that users have different travel needs the site is still able to offer products that cater for almost all travel requirements.

Products and Services

In 2005, teletextholidays.co.uk launched a new integrated hotel search, giving users access to over 100,000 hotels worldwide. The comprehensive search facility complements the successful flights product and features accommodation from around the world. A new search function allows customers to search for hotels, apartments or villas. Users can also select the number of people per room and display prices for the entire holiday duration rather than per night, as is the case with many other sites.

In addition to thousands of holiday offers, teletextholidays.co.uk also provides a unique range of other services like, for instance, Destination Guides. These give an up-front, unbiased account of a

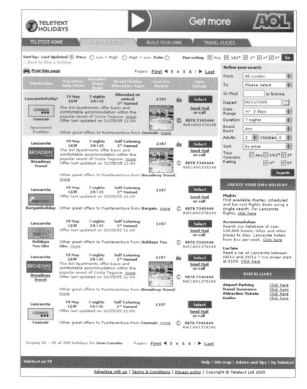

variety of destinations, in the UK and overseas, as well as cruise-ship, port and ski resort guides.

teletextholidays.co.uk customers are able to search and compare deals on: holidays, flights and accommodation, ski deals, cruises, UK breaks, short breaks, car-hire and tickets for popular attractions.

With seven million searches, made by over 3.4 million visitors per month, teletextholidays.co.uk has a unique Holiday Offers Database (HOD) where consumers can search for worldwide holidays from

HISTORY

1996 – *Teletext publishes its first website, with a holidays section included alongside the News and Sports results.*

1999 – *Teletext launches its Holiday Offers Database and associated entry tools for the UK trade.*

2001 – *teletextholidays.co.uk launches as a stand-alone website, offering predominantly package holidays. Ski Channel and Cruise Channel are also introduced.*

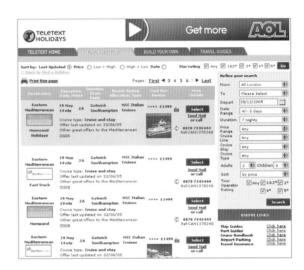

advertising travel agents. HOD allows users to view more content from holiday brochures and search by way of star ratings or view the most recent holiday offers loaded onto the site – similar in principal to search engines but without the issues related to checking positioning or bids.

The new Special Interest Channel appeals to those looking for holidays that promise something different or simply an active, adventurous, or sporty break, while the Stag and Hen section caters for those looking to organise the perfect pre-nuptial party night. For customers short of inspiration teletextholidays.co.uk offers a 'What's New' section which enables users to search for new ideas, up-and-coming resorts and tips from seasoned travel writers.

Personality and Goals

The Teletext Holiday brand has always stood for offering users unbiased access to great value deals, from hundreds of the UK's top travel brands. This holds true online as much as on TV. The brand aims to inspire and inform customers with its reliable, friendly and direct personality. Future plans include the launch of a next generation website, which will add more intuitive search facilities to enable users to get exactly what they want more quickly.

www.teletextholidays.co.uk

2003 – teletextholidays.co.uk's integrated flights search launches, aggregating flight deals from multiple suppliers.

2004 – A redesigned website addresses the growth in independent bookings. It includes improved flight, accommodation and car-hire functionality.

2005 – Further site modifications ensue.

89

THOMSON Local.com™

Market Context

The average consumer is increasingly well versed in how to obtain data and wants speedy access to that information through a variety of different search formats: print, online, mobile phones and digital television. Businesses are responding to this demand by becoming more 'multi-channel' in their route to servicing and reaching potential customers in the most cost effective way.

With more than 35 million people – 60% of the population – online in the UK and 191 million searches for businesses and services every month, ThomsonLocal.com is both a leading source of information for consumers and a powerful advertising medium for businesses.

Within the internet search market competition for consumer usage and business advertising is fierce. A major contributing factor to ThomsonLocal.com's market prominence is its expanding search partner network that includes, Google™, Tiscali and Yahoo! UK and Ireland.

Achievements

Thomson Directories, publishers of the online directory and the Thomson Local print directories, are a 2005 Business Superbrand, recognised for their energy in predicting market demands and responding to consumer needs – they were also named one of the top employers by the 2005 Sunday Times Best Companies to Work for League Table.

ThomsonLocal.com and its partner network generate 15 million page impressions a month and more than 200 million monthly searches across the WebFinder network.

Thomsonlocal.com was the first online directory to launch a 'pay as you go' advertising package and to offer free website links and email contact forms to all of its business listings. It was also the first to provide a comprehensive lifestyle section with easy-to-access local and national information, to accommodate today's changing lifestyle needs.

Products and Services

Thomson Directories began operating in 1980 and today produce 173 editions of the Thomson Local, distributing 22 million copies nationwide. All this information, and more, is available on ThomsonLocal.com. Every week Thomson Local directories are used by six million people and generate 15 million business referrals.

ThomsonLocal.com provides modern consumers speedy online access to a range of businesses and services that enable them to locate what they are looking for.

ThomsonLocal.com encourages users to make informed choices by regularly upgrading its content and increasing the range and flexibility of online information access. Improvements in usability and an increased audience for business advertisers, via other major search engines, have contributed to these enhancements.

HISTORY

1980 – Thomson Directories established as an independent publisher of local directories and spend the next two decades building up a reputation as a leading market brand.

2000 – Thomson is acquired by SEAT Pagine Gialle – leading European publisher of telephone directories.

2002 – ThomsonLocal.com goes live, offering easily navigable search routes: UK Business Finder, My Local Area and Search Nearby.

ThomsonLocal.com has an easy-to-navigate homepage, featuring a variety of lifestyle channels that provide users with area specific information including a Restaurant Finder, Cinema Guide and property information. All users can receive an opt-in quarterly e-newsletter to keep them informed of local services and activities.

ThomsonLocal.com uses a number of innovative modifications to simplify the information search process for users. For instance, the Cinema Guide is unique in that it allows users to search solely by film title, as well as displaying times and certifications. Similarly, with the Restaurant Finder users can choose an eatery based on cuisine type and locate the nearest one within a defined geographical area.

Personality and Goals

ThomsonLocal.com benefits from the strength of the Thomson Local brand, which has a proven 25-year track record of helping businesses to expand and for providing information to people – in print and online – relevant to their search.

Thomson Directories seek to innovate, yet still remain a dependable, helpful and reliable brand that provides tailored information in convenient and accessible mediums.

As the online directory has evolved and developed the 'goes further than you think' addition encompasses ThomsonLocal.com's increased awareness and functionality, adding a new dimension to the directory's brand positioning.

www.ThomsonLocal.com

THINGS YOU DIDN'T KNOW...

Restaurants are one of the most searched for headings on ThomsonLocal.com.

People are going Greek – the number of Greek restaurants listed has increased proportionately more than any other type.

The original blue Thomson cat came from a rescue centre.

ThomsonLocal.com displays nearly one million maps to users every month.

2003 – WebFinder.com launches 'pay as you go' advertising, enabling businesses to promote websites using search engines to drive sales enquiries.

2004 – LocalPlus launches featuring a number of lifestyle channels, Restaurant Finder also launches as well as Cinema Guide.

2005 – Thomson Directories becomes the first European directory publisher authorised to sell advertising that appears on Google™ AdWords®.

2005 – Introduces a range of marketing packages that guarantee response to advertising for small and medium sized businesses.

TIMES ONLINE

Market Context

The market in online news provision is as competitive today as any other media format. With costs for starting a news-orientated website relatively low, and providers unrestricted by geography or Government licensing, competition stems from: portals, newspapers, broadcasters and citizen publishing.

Despite the proliferation of cheap news content on the web, both 'old' and 'new' brands dominate the Nation's news-reading habits. The growing demand for quality online news, that values authenticity, integrity and trust, has enabled recognised offline brands to transfer readily to the internet.

With Times Online, readers expect content, as with its offline brands, to be engaging, accurate and written by top-class journalists and commentators.

In the UK, the top 20 news sites account for 81% of all news readership (Source: Comscore Media Metrix) – every one of these a recognised news or online brand. It is within this highly competitive marketplace that Times Online contributes to the way millions of Britons consume online news every day.

Achievements

Times Online increased its initial number of users by adopting a series of major online and in-paper marketing pushes.

The strategy was successful and by 2004, Times Online was attracting 19 million page impressions – 1.8 million unique users – every month. Just 12 months later this increased to 42.8 million page impressions – five million unique monthly users – and by September 2005 Times Online was registering 65 million page impressions – 6.5 million unique users – a staggering growth of 260% in just 16 months (Source: WebSideStory's HBX).

In October 2005 independent research, from the British Business Survey, confirmed that Times Online and its print versions, The Times and The Sunday Times, rated number one choice for business with Times Online overtaking FT.com and guardian.co.uk as the most popular website for all business consumers.

Thanks to a combination of strong editorial principles and a close understanding of the needs of readers and advertisers Times Online now exceeds revenue targets and overall market growth.

Products and Services

Times Online provides a strong independent breaking news team to deliver intra-day coverage of top news stories and events.

Editorially the site is an innovator in news-breaking methods; it introduced blogging into mainstream reporting, expanded business news and data and launched tailored sections such as Women, Technology and Internet and Debate.

Times Online draws on the vast experience of renowned newspaper writers and big-name columnists and specialists – like Gerard Baker, US Editor of The Times – who regularly contribute to the site as eyewitnesses for emerging world news events.

HISTORY

1995 – thetimes.co.uk and sunday-times.co.uk launch as two separate static websites, covering the news content of the respective papers.

2000 – The online editorial teams are combined, although two separate websites remain. Both sites undergo a complete redesign and change in architecture.

2002 – The two sites are unified and a single commercial operating business is formed for Times Online.co.uk.

2002 – Times Online becomes the first UK national newspaper to launch an E-paper for overseas nationals.

For commercially sponsored projects, Times Online has created innovative packages for clients, such as, downloadable guides to digital photography and offbeat feature material for marketing.

An expanded business news section offers markets and stock news to rival competitor's sites, strongly supported by share and markets data that gives users a clear 'dashboard', with interactive displays.

The Debate section of The Times is now online providing users with a deep forum for discussion. In June 2005 The Times also moved all of its listings online, creating a powerful symbiotic online arm of The Knowledge Weekly Entertainment Magazine.

Personality and Goals

By carrying the heritage of two of the world's oldest surviving newspapers Times Online bears

TIMESONLINE
Great New Business Idea?

a responsibility to users to deliver content objectively and with integrity. As a brand Times Online seeks to introduce emerging subjects, news and innovations to web savvy users, with a definite degree of authority and authenticity. Its personality is conscientious and stable, whilst remaining assertive, practical and well informed.

www.timesonline.co.uk

2003 – Times Online launches premium classified search products in Appointments and Motoring.

2004 – Times Online becomes one of the first newspaper websites to announce its first profitable quarter. Times Online removes its overseas subscription charge, opening its doors to a worldwide audience.

2005 – The Business section goes from strength to strength; incorporating stock market portfolios for investors, interactive market charts and live market commentary.

tiscali.

Market Context

Broadband internet access has taken off in a big way in the UK. According to 2005 research from Nielsen//NetRatings, 72% of Britons access the internet from home using broadband, compared to 46% in 2004. Users' demand for faster and richer online experiences is fuelling intense competition amongst leading broadband providers, such as Tiscali, BT, Yahoo! and AOL. Other communication companies are getting in on the broadband act, such as BSkyB and Orange, which is replacing the Wanadoo name in the UK.

Connection speeds have grown to meet burgeoning consumer demand, with what were once premium broadband services of 1Mb, now marketed as standard. In 2004, only 9% of the UK population had broadband of over 512K, but in late 2005 that figure leapt to over 44%. Simultaneously, in a trend spearheaded by Tiscali, the price of broadband has rapidly fallen.

This explosion in broadband usage has transformed the way that people use the web, with more video and music streaming, gaming, and 'podcasting', involving downloading TV and radio programmes to handheld devices such as iPods.

Achievements

In just seven years, Tiscali has grown to become the largest independent ISP in Europe.

It is a company that has revolutionised and accelerated the broadband market, especially in the UK, where it established two key landmarks

– broadband for under £20 and then a broadband service for the same price as unmetered dial-up access, at £15.99.

Backed by a major advertising campaign in 2004, the timing of this launch was perfect, as the UK broadband market blossomed. Tiscali was perfectly positioned to benefit. The move also established Tiscali as the 'consumer champion' ISP.

The combination of product innovation, revitalised branding and high-profile marketing, catapulted Tiscali forward and by the end of 2004 it had trebled its UK broadband customers to over 300,000, growing to 800,000 in 2005.

Tiscali's unique approach has made a strong impression on consumers, journalists and analysts, with Tiscali recognised as a catalyst for more choice and competitively priced broadband. The Financial Times described Tiscali as: "A good provider of cheaper broadband, which is always good for the consumer," while The Mirror called Tiscali "the biggest innovator in the consumer broadband market".

The company has won numerous influential awards, including the 2003 Deloitte Fast 500 award for the fastest growing technology company in Europe, Best ISP in the 2003 Internet Made Easy awards and Best Pay As You Go Provider in the 2004 ISPA Awards.

Products and Services

Tiscali UK provides a full range of broadband and dial-up packages which still set the market standard for price and performance. It also provides telephony packages, with its Smart Talk range.

HISTORY

1998 – *Tiscali is established in Sardinia as a regional telecoms operator by founder Renato Soru.*

1999 – *The company establishes the free internet model and expands across Italy. Tiscali floats in October 1999 and begins expanding across Europe.*

2000 – *Tiscali buys the Dutch ISP World Online for £1.7 billion, in a deal which makes it Europe's third largest ISP.*

2001 – *Tiscali buys France's second-biggest ISP, Liberty Surf, for £408 million, Line One in the UK for £62 million and SurfEU for £47 million*

Tiscali is also exploring new product possibilities, such as Voice Over IP (VoIP) music and video streaming, movies on demand, and TV over the internet.

In music it was the first company in the UK to offer a legal music download service, launching over a year before iTunes first arrived in the UK. This service now offers over 750,000 tracks.

THINGS YOU DIDN'T KNOW...

▌ **The Tiscali name comes from the Tiscali Caves, close to the home of the company in Cagliary, Sardinia.**

▌ **Tiscali was the first to launch a free internet service in Italy.**

▌ **Tiscali is the official online sponsor of 46664 – the Nelson Mandela Foundation's Aids awareness campaign.**

The company also supports new bands, through the Tiscali Showcase, and connects fans with music through webcasts and sessions, including exclusive VIP material from the Reading Festival in 2005.

Tiscali is also increasingly active in film and entertainment. In 2005, it launched tiscali.tv, a dedicated broadband channel featuring entertainment content including music videos, interviews, sport, animation, film trailers and short films. In film, it has launched Tiscali Cinema, providing video on demand over broadband. This is an online home movie download service, but it also carries new content, such as the film EMR, which received the world's first simultaneous triple platform release – online at Tiscali, in Cinemas and on DVD.

Personality and Goals

Tiscali has a mission to champion fair and equal access to the internet, empowering users, challenging the status quo and acting in spirit with the founding democratic spirit of the web. It is committed to introducing advanced and original ideas, and bringing these through the internet to everyone. Overarching everything it does, is an attitude of constant attention and social responsibility towards the internet and its users as well as a dedication to delivering the best online experience, through convention-busting innovation.

www.tiscali.co.uk

003 – Tiscali rocks the UK ernet market by launching oadband for the price of dial-up, £15.99 per month.

2004 – Tiscali begins the sale of its operations in eight smaller countries, deciding to focus on Italy, UK, Netherlands and Germany. These countries contribute over 95% of the group revenue, with the UK alone now contributing over 40%.

2005 – Tiscali UK upgrades services to focus on 1 and 2Mb services only, but retaining a market leading £14.99 price point. Online the Tiscali portal focuses strongly on Entertainment with the launch of tiscali.tv and Tiscali Cinema and invests further in the support of live music.

TOPSHOP

Market Context

Responding quickly to emerging trends has been a key success factor for retailers such as Topshop, which has carved out a reputation for its ability to pre-empt the latest catwalk styles at affordable prices and with the shortest possible lead times.

The UK market for women's clothing is forecast to grow by almost 10% between 2003 and 2008 to reach a value of nearly £12.8 billion. Tops will remain the largest sector contributing a value of £2.9 billion by the year 2008, accounting for almost 23% of value sector share (Source: Euromonitor).

Achievements

Topshop has undergone a transformation since the mid 1990s, blossoming from 'cheap and cheerful' for the nation's teenagers to a seriously cool, trendsetting brand.

It has become a high street retail phenomenon, enjoying a huge growth in sales and creating a distinctive personality with an individual brand mix. It continues to headline in nearly every fashion title and broadsheet, establishing a reputation for bringing innovation and style to the high street.

Topshop has become a multi-award-winning brand, carrying off numerous industry gongs. Most recently, it won Customer Service Initiative of the Year for its new Topshop To Go service at the Retail Week Awards 2005. The past year has also seen it win awards from magazines including Company, In Style and Time Out.

The driving force behind the transformation of Topshop is the team led by brand director Jane Shepherdson, who has been rated as one of the fashion industry's most influential figures. As well as the expertise of buyers and designers, the team relies on gut instinct to introduce elements they feel are right for the brand. With 300 UK stores and a further 67 international stores, this is a philosophy that seems to be paying dividends.

Products and Services

The Topshop website is a key element of the brand's strategy. Having started from a back room in Topshop's flagship store at Oxford Circus with just one person picking and dispatching orders from the store's stock room, this has all changed.

April 2005 saw www.Topshop.com launch its new look, with must-have products on the home page, a most-wanted item updated daily and limited edition pieces available from flagship stores. Now, the site is updated every week with more than 100 new products.

HISTORY

1964 – Topshop launched by parent company, The Arcadia Group, which dates back to 1900.

1974 – Topshop sets up as a standalone retailer, catering for 13-25 year-olds.

1978 – A boys' and young men's version, Topman, is introduced and in 1982, Top Girl, for 9-14 year-olds, arrives.

To maximise the popularity of the site, Topshop communicates every week with its loyal customer database of 150,000 subscribers through the Style Notes newsletter informing them of everything new on the site. Response rates are up to 25%, showing that the Style Notes are an eagerly awaited weekly event for online shoppers.

Personality and Goals

Topshop is a fashion emporium that blends cutting-edge style with affordability. Loved by fashionistas, models and celebrities alike, Topshop has evolved into a fashion label that epitomises up-to-the-minute affordable fashion.

Topshop has earned celebrity endorsement, reflecting its reputation as a high street fashion Mecca.

At the core of the brand is a respect for creativity and innovation in every form. Creativity is the engine that fuels the success of Topshop.

www.Topshop.com

toptable.co.uk
free online restaurant & party booking

Market Context

Having pioneered online restaurant booking, toptable.co.uk is now the largest service of its kind in Europe, fulfilling more than 50% of all restaurant reservations made online in the UK. In 2006, toptable anticipate to seat 1.5 million diners, generating over £50 million of the restaurant industry. Online restaurant booking is still very much in its infancy and the biggest challenge is encouraging consumers to make the move from telephone to web bookings.

Today toptable makes reservations on behalf of thousands of restaurants in the UK, Dublin, Paris and Barcelona and has aggressive global expansion plans to create a toptable presence in many other cities including New York, Tokyo, Moscow, Hong Kong, Beijing, Sydney, Cape Town and other key global destinations.

Consumers can book for every occasion, from an intimate dinner for two at a Michelin-starred restaurant to a casual supper at a local neighbourhood pizza place. The specialist events division make reservations for parties up to several thousand and work with many major corporations.

Achievements

As the first online restaurant booking service in the UK, toptable is an innovative concept for both restaurants and diners. Just a few months

after the launch of the service, in June 2000, its founder Karen Hanton was awarded the Financial Times/Möet Hennessey Extraordinary Achievers Award for the toptable idea. Four years later, Hanton was named one of the Top 100 Most Influential People in the First Decade of the Internet in an NOP/e-consultancy poll.

In July 2003 the toptable site received the Web User Gold Award for Favourite Website and six months later was awarded 'Lifestyle Website of the Year' by Internet Magazine. In February 2005 toptable was named as the 17th fastest-growing new media company in the influential Media Momentum Awards.

HISTORY

February 2000 – *toptable.co.uk launches as a marketing tool for the highly fragmented restaurant industry, with eminent shareholders including legendary football manager Sir Alex Ferguson and celebrity chef Gary Rhodes.*

June 2000 – *toptable's events booking service launches.*

March 2001 – *toptable sets up a major partnership with Club Nokia, with the toptable service bookmarked on every handset.*

April 2002 – *toptable launches its VIP club.*

Sir Alex Ferguson trained as a chef and intended to open a restaurant in Paisley. He didn't get planning permission and decided to have a go at football management instead.

Monthly visitors to the toptable website would fill the Albert Hall at least 125 times.

toptable devotees who earn enough loyalty points can choose to have Gary Rhodes personally cook for them and three of their friends.

Products and Services

toptable is a lifestyle tool that aims to revolutionise how people today make restaurant reservations. It is a fast, reliable and free service for both business and leisure occasions and has created a unique dining community. It gives the inside track and inspiration on where to eat out, and features hundreds of special offers at any one time. It also enables users to follow up-to-the-minute trends and aims to keep them ahead of the game regarding restaurant-related news and gossip.

toptable has thousands of bookable restaurants across the UK, Dublin, Paris and Barcelona; and for each of these consumers can access: 360° restaurant views; sample menus; location maps; unique feedback and dynamic ratings from people who have actually dined there; a leading industry loyalty programme; 'top rewards' allowing consumers to collect points and eat out for free; and location-based mobile-phone booking.

Personality and Goals

toptable is an innovation-led brand that aims to think and do things differently. It inspires and enables its users to get the most out of eating and drinking in restaurants. toptable is fun and edgy, yet warm and sociable.

www.toptable.co.uk

August 2003 – Diageo, the world's leading drinks business, becomes a toptable.co.uk shareholder.

January 2004 – Launch of unique diner feedback, featuring comments only from people who have actually eaten at the restaurants.

June 2004 – toptable launches its loyalty programme 'top rewards'.

November 2004 – toptable seats its millionth diner.

2005 – The Launch of 'Destination Paris', is closely followed by the launch of 'Destination Barcelona'.

Market Context

In the five years since its inception, totaljobs.com has built its position as one of the leading job boards in the UK recruitment marketplace.

Totaljobs.com is part of Totaljobs Group Ltd, which is owned by Reed Elsevier plc.

The site caters for a wide range of recruiters, from larger multinationals to small regionally-based businesses, to recruitment consultants and recruitment advertising agencies.

Totaljobs' jobseekers come from all areas of the UK, all industries and all functional roles. It has around one million unique users visiting the site each month, with a jobseeker applying for a job every six seconds.

Achievements

With more than 1,500 customers placing 70,000 vacancies at any one time, totaljobs is the UK's fastest-growing online recruitment business. Its clients include GlaxoSmithKline, B&Q, AstraZeneca, P&O, T-Mobile, Carlsberg Tetley, PricewaterhouseCoopers, IBM, Carphone Warehouse and The Royal Bank of Scotland.

Totaljobs' achievements over the past year include the development of an award-winning seminar programme and becoming the first recruitment site in the UK to carry out an ABCe audited diversity survey amongst its jobseekers. Totaljobs was voted the Most Popular Generic Recruitment Site by alljobsuk in 2004.

Products and Services

Totaljobs.com is a recruitment site offering fast access for jobseekers to the latest UK jobs. It aims to understand how pressurised job hunting

HISTORY

2000 – Totaljobs established online.

2002 – Totaljobs revenue increases by 79% year-on-year.

2003 – Totaljobs makes an exclusive partnership with MSN to power the MSN jobs channel.

November 2003 – The Network, a European recruitment alliance is co-founded by Totaljobs.com and Stepstone. Today The Network has an alliance with the leading job sites from more than 50 offices in 32 countries enabling recruiters to attract global talent to their UK or overseas vacancies.

100

can be, so its focus is on providing slick candidate tools and relevant careers advice. Through surveying its consumers frequently and inviting feedback, it has fostered an open two-way dialogue that is based on trust.

Totaljobs offers job posting, CV database search and employer branding. Totaljobs direct is a service by which employers can post a job instantly using a credit card, while the Totaljobs' network helps UK recruiters to fill overseas vacancies across 32 countries.

Its extensive eDM programme has proved invaluable to its audience which reports back to the site on the career successes they have had via totaljobs.com.

It is over-representative of ethnic minorities within the UK and preferred by urban careerists, typically generating more than 500,000 online job applications per month for its recruiters.

Personality and Goals

A pioneering, educational, secure, customer-facing and inclusive brand, Totaljobs takes pride in having held on where others have failed. Totaljobs is determined to evolve and thrive in a volatile and changing market.

Totaljobs aims to understand the online recruitment market and wants to educate its customers so that they too can appreciate this method of recruitment. Totaljobs believes its responsibility goes beyond

selling advertising, towards evangelizing and opening people's eyes to a new way of recruiting and jobseeking.

Totaljobs knows that to thrive it must continue to embrace a diverse market, appealing to jobseekers with a wide range of skills, education, abilities or background.

www.totaljobs.com

UpMyStreet »

Market Context

UpMyStreet aims to be the leading online resource for local area information. The site competes in various online markets, including the online property market, local search engine technology, which saw the arrival of Google Local in April 2005, and switching services, dominated by UpMyStreet's parent company, uSwitch. As a one-stop-shop for local area information – from crime figures to school guides to what properties are actually sold for – UpMyStreet remains unique.

The defining characteristics of today's internet marketplace include information overload and media fragmentation. To counter information overload, UpMyStreet aims to give people not just the information required to make a decision, but also the tools with which to action it, through the capabilities provided by uSwitch. Furthermore, UpMyStreet's localised message boards are a distinct advantage in a marketplace where consumers seeking information are

increasingly turning from conventional sources (such as the press) to fellow consumers via online communities.

Achievements

UpMyStreet has been '…made famous for being able to tell you just about everything you needed to know about a postcode, from the price of houses to the local MP', wrote The Guardian in January 2003. Indeed, the site has been awarded many accolades since its 1999 consumer launch, including being voted one of 'Europe's Top 100 Internet Ventures' by The Sunday Times E-League in July 2000 and winning the Best Use of the Web award at the New Media Age Awards in 2001.

Products and Services

Together, the various products and services on UpMyStreet provide a full picture of a postcode. This enables users to make decisions about their home or local area – from where to live, to the best broadband supplier. The integration of uSwitch's online switching functionality has been an integral step in UpMyStreet's campaign to become not just about getting information, but about making decisions online.

HISTORY

October 1998
– UpMyStreet goes live on the web as a technology showcase, not a consumer website. By Christmas 1998, it has half a million users.

April 1999 –
UpMyStreet launches as a limited company, backed by family and friends.

April 2000 – UpMyStreet receives £12 million in funding from News International and Continuation Investments NV.

September 2001 – UpMyStreet wins a deal to provide services to internet kiosks in Post Offices.

Some of the services available from UpMyStreet include: FindMyNearest…™, a local business and services search engine; actual property prices, which tells users exactly what a property sold for; switching services for energy, home phone or broadband services; along with property, school, transport and local news services.

Personality and Goals

UpMyStreet was launched by a few inspired developers who had been up late thinking about geo-coding and the web. The passion behind the technology was infectious however and users came to the site in droves as news spread of the arrival

This Month We Love: London

of a new idea on the web. The site soon had iconic status and a place close to the hearts of web leaders and enthusiasts alike.

With no brand management to speak of, UpMyStreet grew up over the next few years from a great piece of technology into a forward-thinking, impartial, friendly site, much loved for its no-nonsense design and for putting users at the heart of everything it did. UpMyStreet continues today with its original goal – to arm individuals and neighbourhoods with the information and tools they need to make decisions about their home lives and communities.

It aims to be the expert users consult when they want to move home, choose a good school, contact their council, set up a school run or find their nearest florist. It is also the embodiment of its users – a neighbourhood of its own, with a unique knowledge base and flavour.

www.upmystreet.com

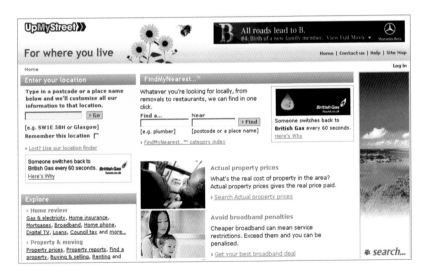

Market Context

What Car? aims to be unique among motoring titles in providing expert, impartial advice on all aspects of car buying. While other motoring websites are aiming at enthusiasts and some promote their own personalities, What Car? works hard to put the car buyer first and has the simple aim of helping them buy better.

Among motoring websites, Auto Trader is by far the biggest, but it has a very different aim: it's a classified ads service. Top Gear is a dominant brand on TV and on the bookstalls, but its online offering is not as well-developed. What Car?'s other competitors include Autoexpress.co.uk and Channel 4's 4Car.

Achievements

What Car? is consistently placed in the top 10 of more than 3,000 automotive websites, as ranked by Hitwise, and achieves 10 million page impressions and 700,000 users a month.

In 2002 the Association of Online Publishers (AOP) awarded What Car? Best Consumer Website of the Year before awarding it with Best Consumer Publisher of the Year a year later.

In 2004, What Car? was shortlisted for the AOP consumer website of the year and consumer publisher of the year.

Products and Services

The prime goal of What Car? is to help the consumer buy the right car at the right price. Core to this are two pieces of information: road tests and target prices.

Its nine-point tests are developments of tests that What Car? magazine has been carrying out since its launch in 1973. The starting point for each evaluation is the consumer and what their demands are from a particular type of car. What Car? offers a clear verdict on the nine major attributes of a new car, with a clear overall star rating.

HISTORY

1997 – www.whatcar.com launches as an online authority on all aspects of car buying.

2001 – What Car? introduces the nine-point road test for all new cars on sale in the UK.

2002 – www.whatcar.com is appointed motoring content provider for AOL and Autotrader.

2002 – What Car? introduces the nine-point road test for used cars.

2003 – Annual revenues of www.whatcar.com exceed £1 million.

What Car?'s Target Price was launched in 2000 and remains a true indication of discounts available in car showrooms. Each month What Car? carries out thousands of mystery shopping tests to determine a Target Price for every model available.

What Car? also stands behind the Target Price in the form of the Target Price Promise – if a dealer won't match its Target Price, it will put the customer in touch with one who will. Target Prices are updated on a weekly basis.

Additional content on What Car? includes daily news updates covering new models and motoring issues, special features ranging from security super-tests to coverage from major international motorshows and clear advice on how consumers can get a good deal.

Two recent innovations stand out: reader reviews and video tests. What Car? now has nearly 4,000 readers' reviews of cars they have driven, giving users an additional source of information in addition to the What Car? verdict.

What Car? also has more than 150 video tests online. These have been designed to give a clear view of the car on the move and in the studio, with voiceovers talking the user through the major points of the car. These are designed to be factual and informative rather than entertaining.

Personality and Goals

One phrase comes up repeatedly when people are asked about What Car? They describe it simply as 'the car buyer's bible'. A quarter of all new car buyers refer to What Car? while they're making their buying decision.

www.whatcar.com

THINGS YOU DIDN'T KNOW...

More than £7 billion of new cars are sold on What Car?'s recommendation each year.

What Car? is part of Haymarket Publishing, the UK's largest privately-owned publishing company, owned by former deputy prime minister Lord Heseltine.

What Car? was launched in 1973 when the cheapest new car on sale was the Bond Bug at £619. Today, the cheapest new car What Car? lists is the £4,795 Perodua Kelisa.

2003 – The first What Car? video road test is produced. The car under scrutiny is the Ford Mondeo.

2003 – www.whatcar.com reaches five million page impressions.

2004 – The 100th video road test is produced by www.whatcar.com.

2004 – www.whatcar.com reaches seven million page impressions.

2005 – The first live motor show webcast, from the prestigious Geneva Motor Show, takes place on www.whatcar.com.

2005 – www.whatcar.com annual revenues exceed £2 million.

YELL.COM

Market Context

The growth of the internet in recent years has resulted in it playing an important role in today's society. Consumers rely on the internet to find information they need and businesses recognise the value of the internet as an effective marketing tool.

Yell.com launched almost a decade ago and provides businesses and services with an effective online advertising solution, as well as enabling consumers to find information and contact details for businesses and services. Yell.com has rapidly grown to become a leading UK local search engine and major online advertising medium with a database that features around two million UK business listings including more than 150,000 searchable advertisers.

Yell.com is a key part of Yell's portfolio in the UK and supports its aim to be the best information bridge between buyers and sellers in its markets, regardless of channel, time or location. Yell is a leading international directories business, which operates in the classified advertising market through printed, online and telephone-based media.

Achievements

Yell.com is now the fastest growing arm of Yell in the UK, with an increase in turnover of just over 40% to £36.2 million in the financial year ending March 31st 2005. This growth reflects an increase in searchable advertisers which in September 2005 stood at 159,000 – more than 31% increase from September 2004.

Its profit, measured by EBITDA, rose by more than 80% in the last financial year to £9.6 million, from £5.3 million the year before.

Products and Services

Once a consumer has found a suitable business or service on Yell.com, they can plot a route with a map and either walking or driving directions to the selected business. Yell.com can also provide the location and price guide for the nearest car parks.

Yell.com's location thesaurus contains more than 40,000 locations, enabling consumers to search anywhere in the UK by postcode, town

HISTORY

1996 – Yell.co.uk launches as an online directory for UK businesses, shops and services.

2000 – Yell.co.uk re-launches as Yell.com.

2001 – Yell.com introduces a WAP (Wireless Application Protocol) service enabling access to its database via the internet from a mobile phone.

2003 – Yell.com text launches, providing business information in text format to a mobile phone.

2004 – www.yelldirect.co launches – a new online sale and account management system.

or county. Consumers can even search using London tube stations or national parks.

Yell.com's database is available through mobile phone technology – via text, WAP or JAVA™ technology.

Yell.com mobile presents Yell.com on the consumer's handset through JAVA™ and other advanced technology, enabling them to enter search requests and connect directly to its business database.

Yell.com offers businesses a range of advertising options from a direct link to their website via a 'Web Link' to a 'Site Builder' which enables them to build and manage their own website. Alternatively, an 'Enhanced Listing' enables those without a website to provide searchable information about their business.

Yell's online sales and account service www.yelldirect.com allows companies to buy advertising, update products and manage their account at any time.

Yell.com can also provide usage statistics to advertisers, to prove the value of their advertising and demonstrate that their investment is good value for money.

Personality and Goals

Yell.com is a major online brand with a modern, authoritative personality and simple, versatile and responsive brand values. Yell.com is more than just an online directory because as well as finding what they

want, when they want it, consumers have access to a number of additional features including links to websites, maps and directions plus detailed consumer advice.

www.yell.com

Unravelling Brand Value

A paper prepared by Jane Piper of Jane Piper Brand Strategy Consultancy on behalf of The Superbrands organisation

JANE PIPER

Independent Consultant
www.janepiperbrandstrategy.co.uk

Jane Piper is an independent consultant with specialist expertise in creating, managing and developing brand value for large, medium and small organisations.

She has 20 years consultancy experience gained both in-house and independently, focusing on the strategic development and management of brands, for clients across key market sectors such as travel and leisure, financial services, the public sector, energy, food and drink.

Her clients are wide and diverse, and have included both market leaders as well as medium-sized businesses, all of whom have an interest in understanding and maximising the value and return on investment in their brands.

Since RHM first placed a balance sheet value on their key brands in 1988 and the London Stock Exchange endorsed the concept in 1989 (allowing the inclusion of intangible assets in class tests for shareholder approvals during takeovers), the door has opened for companies to value their brands and include them as intangible assets on their balance sheet.

However, the issue of exactly how to value brands has been the subject of much debate ever since.

Despite subsequent recognition in the finance department that brands are valuable assets with many useful attractions, often making a significant contribution to the total value of a company, the lack of consistency and clarity in approach to valuing them has contributed towards confusion particularly in the marketing community.

As brand guardians, it is no longer good enough to understand what constitutes a brand, we need to know how to calculate their worth, and to adopt branding strategies to develop and maximise their value potential.

The purpose of this paper is to provide an independent and introductory overview to valuing brands for the benefit of the marketing community, as well as to provide some clarity on the differing methodologies that are used to calculate their value.

It has been compiled independently in conjunction with the co-operation of a number of leading brand valuation practitioners, to whom we are grateful for their time and contribution in furthering the cause of branding.

Brands - Valuable Assets

As brands are often a company's most important and valuable intangible asset, particularly in certain market sectors, the subject regularly fills column inches in the business pages of the national press and other journals as the debate rumbles on about how to value them.

Intangibles are now accounting for an ever-increasing % of market value, approximately 60% across the FTSE All Share Index – up from only 10% some 50 years ago (PricewaterhouseCoopers (PwC) Research, Intellectual Asset Management 2003).

Later research shows that in the US merger and acquisition market in 2003, some 48% of corporate value was placed on brands and intangibles (PwC Research US 2004).

Historically, it is those businesses with strong brands that commanded a higher share price, as demonstrated by the following chart:

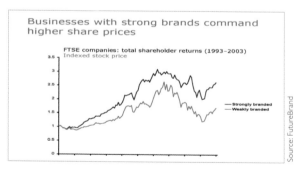

Businesses with strong brands command higher share prices

FTSE companies: total shareholder returns (1993-2003)
Indexed stock price

Source: FutureBrand

In addition, the current rise in trademark applications in the US & UK (following the blip in numbers as the dot.com bubble burst post 2000) demonstrates the continuing trend in launching new brands – and the creation of whole new brand-led markets.

For example, US lawyers Decherts quote almost four new 'carb' related brands being posted daily in the US for trademark status at the height of the Atkins publicity in 2004.

With new brands in new sectors and new delivery technologies, it is not surprising that there is increased interest in realising the power and value of the brand outside of the traditional consumer arena in sectors such as banking, energy and transport.

"A powerful brand adds value to all the assets a company has – product and package features and benefits, manufacturing plants, employees, customer relationships, marketing, promotions. With a powerful brand every relevant econometric can be, and should be, more productive."

AT Kearney

Along with the rise in importance of brand value since its conception there has been much focus on determining more precise, rigorous and robust methods to calculate value:

"The valuation debate has moved on considerably since the advent of Interbrand's methodology and its focus on the capital base of a company when determining brand value.

Brand valuation may be an art but it is becoming a more sophisticated art."

Gravitas

But whilst the brand valuation debate continues there is at least wide recognition that the value of a brand can be a significant proportion of total business value.

The damage to a company's brand by the adverse actions of one particular group of stakeholders has the ability to inflict serious harm to its reputation, and wipe millions off its market value as was demonstrated most vividly with Arthur Anderson.

Today's business environment places Corporate Governance as the number one boardroom issue. The links between governance, trust and reputation are becoming ever closer since Alan Greenspan's famous comments:

"Corporate Reputation is rising out of the ashes of the debacle as a significant economic value."

Chicago, May 2003

To all intents and purposes, a company's corporate brand and reputation is one and the same thing, if anything a brand is seen as something more 'tangible'.

Place a value on your brand – place a value on your reputation has never been more relevant. In addition it is even more important to give greater clarity on the subject of brand value with the introduction of new international accounting standards this year.

Exactly What Is The Brand Asset?

Even the valuation industry itself acknowledges the confusion:

"PwC recognises that there is confusion in the marketplace related to:

- the terminology that is used eg. brand equity/brand value
- the purposes and benefits of brand valuation
- the brand valuation methodologies

Delving deeper, there is even confusion as to what exactly a brand means, particularly in valuation terms. Different people interpret the term differently in different environments.

Establishing clear definitions should be considered fundamental before undertaking a brand valuation exercise.

Brands have been interpreted at its most simple level as the heart of an organisation's visual identity i.e. its name and logo. This is usually protected as a trademark.

At the next level, it includes both trademarks and all forms of intellectual property that go with the brand, including product design, patents and rights, domain names and any other associated visual or verbal communication of the brand.

The widest and fairest assessment of brand for valuation purposes, includes identifying the role of brand within the value chain of the organisation as a whole.

This interpretation has been simplified as:

"the first we refer to as the trademark, the second we refer to as the brand, and the third we refer to as the branded business"

Brand Finance

Whilst there is still confusion and lack of understanding as to what constitutes a brand for valuation purposes, the above definition is largely supported by the practising industry.

For example, Ernst & Young would take a commercial assessment of a business and believe that a brand is created and supported by other functions.

"Taking a typical example, a retail brand is reliant on the quality of its product (from materials to manufacturing, source and supply), its retail design and merchandising, its design team and quality of customer service as well as the strength of its property outsourcing contracts.

All of these interlink to drive value in the brand – if one element fails such as distribution, it will have a negative knock-on effect on the value of the brand."

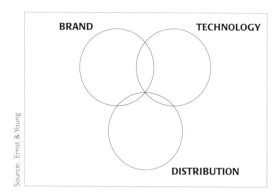

Source: Ernst & Young

BRAND   TECHNOLOGY

DISTRIBUTION

The Requirement To Value

Things are changing ...

2005 sees the introduction of International Financial Reporting Standards (IFRS), designed to bring some uniformity in accounting standards and interpretations around the world.

What does this mean for brands and valuing brands?

Around the world international accounting standards for brands have varied according to the different regulatory standards that are in place in each country.

IFRS will bring some consistency in the overall requirement to value listed-company brands. This includes valuing all brands bought and sold and a requirement for an ongoing annual re-assessment of the value of acquired brands known as an impairment review where the brand does not have a specified useful economic life.

A software brand may for example have a useful economic life applied to it, by the very nature of the rapidly changing technology marketplace, in which case there would not be a need for an annual impairment review. It would, however, need to be depreciated or amortised over the period of its specified economic life.

Corporate brands may or may not have a useful economic life specified and therefore if corporate change has taken place, may be liable for an annual impairment review.

A recent example would be in the acquisition by Spain's Banco Santander of abbey.

Some of these new standards are already in place in certain countries, for example in the US, but what it does mean is consistent international standards on how, why and when brands need to be valued for accounting purposes.

In reality, this will mean that when a company acquires a business, a value will have to be placed on the brand it is acquiring. Surely it makes sense for this information to be used as a basis and benchmark for more targeted and focused brand and marketing strategies to drive greater value out of the brand it is acquiring?

And in addition, if there is a requirement to annually re-assess and monitor value in the form of an impairment review, this provides the ideal opportunity to assess the success or otherwise of marketing strategies and their return on investment. The Board can then use a gain in brand value as an important point in its investor communications on delivering greater shareholder value (although it cannot be revised upwards on the balance sheet).

"For many businesses, the strength of their brands is a key driver of profitability and cash flows. Recognising these assets will reinforce this message to investors and help them judge whether brands are in good health. The accounting requirement to regularly review the value of acquired brands means there will be an ongoing judgement of the success of marketing strategy for investing in brands"

KPMG

What Is In It For Marketing?

"Brand Value is a hot topic for accounting and finance professionals, but an even hotter topic for marketing professionals"

FutureBrand

The big advantage to the Marketing Department is that brand valuation can provide a strong and viable basis to relate the success of its strategy and return on investment to enhanced business performance, which is what the CEO is primarily concerned about. This is particularly relevant where there is big-ticket advertising or significant retail investment.

"The irony is that often a brand is being valued anyway, its just that the marketing department often doesn't know about it, as the finance team may think its not relevant to them - despite the extensive levels of consumer and market-based research that is undertaken, and the strategic insights and options that are identified."

PwC

The issue is how often the finance department and the marketing department realise the potential of the link between statutory financial information being used to shape marketing strategies that deliver superior results.

In reality, there is little crossover between marketing and finance at a strategic level, with the exception of the annual budget rounds, despite the increasing pressure to demonstrate marketing effectiveness.

FutureBrand quote figures from the Marketing Leadership Council that "66% or 2/3rds of its members need to demonstrate financial results of marketing or to show its worth". Superbrands research in 2001 showed that 79% of its members felt that they had adequate metrics/procedures in place to measure marketing effectiveness, 69% brand health and only 44% brand value.

Surely by qualifying and quantifying brand values and demonstrating return on marketing investment marketeers would provide the ultimate evidence of their success?

Why Do Companies Get Brands Valued?

There is common agreement that there are two main reasons why brands get valued:

- Financial Transactions
- Strategic Purposes

The use of brand valuation in **Financial Transactions** is wide and varied and may include:

Tax planning: Transfer of ownership of brands to a more cost-effective tax haven i.e. Switzerland or the Cayman Islands, whereby operating companies are then charged a royalty for the use of the brand. The brand has to be transferred at a market rate requiring commercial validation.

Transfer Pricing: Tax-related or otherwise, where the use of a brand is an integral part of a deal, for example the injection of fresh capital.

Mergers and Acquisitions: Brands have to be valued on merger, acquisition or divestment by listed companies; the premium value placed on intangible assets in particular the brand, often form the heart of the commercial basis of a deal.

In a hostile takeover situation, the value of a brand can often play a key part of a defence to secure a higher valuation.

Security/Securitisation: The value of the brand asset is increasingly being used to provide security particularly in private equity deals, and sometimes in securitisation.

Refinancing/restructuring: Using the value of the brand asset to raise finance, whether for corporate restructuring or for expansion purposes.

Licensing: In either a straightforward financial transaction where licensing is involved, or a situation where a strategic decision may have been taken to license a brand to a third party, its value is fundamental to the deal. This is particular prevalent in the pharmaceutical sector, as well as hotels and entertainment businesses.

Joint Ventures: In setting up and branding a joint venture, particularly between two brand-led businesses possibly in a new market place.

Litigation: In any number of disputes ranging from infringed intellectual property rights and trademark disputes, through to the damage to brand value from the failure of a third-party distribution network.

Investor Relations: To demonstrate the increased worth of the brand and other intangible assets, or the benefits of a brand rationalisation programme and subsequent direct contribution towards improving shareholder value.

There are many **Strategic Reasons** why a brand may need to be valued, including:

Strategic assessment: A changing competitive environment may require re-assessment and the possible re-positioning of a brand.

Corporate restructuring: As an aid to corporate restructuring, particularly in large, diverse international conglomerates.

Brand portfolio management: To review the value in a brand portfolio and to restructure or rationalise brand architecture, based on qualified and quantified consideration of the potential growth, opportunities and risks that exist.

Co-branding: In positioning co-branded ventures, or joint ventures.

New market entry: To understand the brand contribution to the success of a new market entry.

Brand stretch: To explore the 'stretch' potential of a brand.

Global brand management: To assess the performance of localised marketing strategies. This is particularly relevant in international organisations with devolved geographic marketing management structures.

Performance Management: To optimise the effectiveness of marketing and brand strategies through evaluation.

Return on Investment: Analysing the return on brand investment for a variety of reasons, including assessing marketing expenditure and effectiveness.

Brand strategy should today be directly geared towards realising and increasing real value and price premium from brands and as such, be a top-level management issue.

> *"The goal is to increase the value-added potential of the brand towards customers, employees and capital markets"*

> *"Branding is not just about advertising and creativity – it is the discipline of creating value by orchestrating the whole business system towards the brand."*
> The Boston Consulting Group

Not unsurprisingly, it is the Finance Department that drives brand valuation in financial transactions, and either an enlightened CEO or Marketing Director in a strategic situation.

They understand that brands create value in the market and the importance of having a strategy that makes the brand accessible and visible to the customer.

Rarely do the two crossover. **The issue is what is happening in your company?**

> *"The finance director may be after a figure to create greater value in the business, but it is very rare that this is used as a benchmark to guide the strategic development of both brands and marketing strategies to deliver a greater return and enhance value."*
> *Gravitas*

Who Is In The Business Of Valuing Brands?

The companies tend to fall into four main categories:

- The accountancy firms
- Specialist valuation businesses
- Branding businesses with a recognised model in place
- Leading management consultancies

These businesses tend to use methodologies that are recognised by the US Internal Revenue Service and the UK's Inland Revenue, as well as US GAP and International Accounting Standards.

Many other brand-focused and marketing services businesses will offer 'brand value' consulting and may have their own models in place to monitor brand equity or 'value'. It is wise to take independent advice as to whether they are recognised or use robust financial modelling methodologies to realise the value of the brand for dual financial and marketing purposes.

Who Did We Talk To?

For the purposes of this overview we reviewed a range of methodologies and spoke to leading players in this market including:

- Accountancy and professional service firms Ernst & Young, KPMG and PricewaterhouseCoopers.
- Valuation businesses Gravitas and Brand Finance.
- A branding business with a recognised model in place, FutureBrand.
- Management consultancies AT Kearney and The Boston Consulting Group.

The above were happy to contribute as part of a **collective effort** to improve the understanding of brand valuation within the marketing community, and for which we are most grateful for their time and contribution.

This paper is not intended to be an endorsement or otherwise of any one approach to valuing brands, rather an informative overview of the different approaches, contexts and methodologies that are used to calculate brand value.

It is designed to be a practical and helpful initial reference guide to the marketing community on understanding the requirement for and the merits of brand valuation, the different approaches to valuing brands, and the strategic options and practical advantages that arise as a result of understanding the financial value in brands.

Different Types Of Businesses – Different Approaches

The first thing that is apparent is that there is no one common approach to valuing brands, which is why the subject causes such confusion.

Some practitioners advocate a single formulaic approach to valuing brands, whilst others use a variety of valuation methodologies, dependent on the situation or purpose for which they are providing an opinion of value, for example:

Market Value: What someone else is willing to pay for the brand? (Acquisition, Licensing, IFRS)

Value in Current Use: What is the value of the brand asset to the business in its current use? (Tax, Litigation)

Strategic Value: What could the asset be worth going forward – what strategic options are open to maximise value? (Corporate restructuring, Performance Management, Private Equity)

Who Does What

The management consultancies and the branding businesses advocate a single approach to valuing a brand for all situations.

The accounting and valuation businesses may use a number of different methodologies to compare outcomes and determine a broader opinion of value, dependent on the reasons and context for the valuation.

Their logic for this is that it is feasible that the market value of a brand in a transaction situation may be higher than its value-in-use to its existing owner. Clearly it is therefore important to identify the context of the valuation.

> "No single methodology is better than any other, and as a valuer we use as many of the methodologies as possible on any brand.
>
> As with many methodologies, however, it is in their application that the skill lies to ensure that the real economic value of the brands is identified."
>
> Ernst &Young

Broadly-speaking, all the practitioners valued brands for both financial transactions as well as strategic reasons, with the main exception of the management consultancies Boston Consulting Group and AT Kearney, who are primarily concerned with brand valuation as part of a broader strategy review:

> "Brand Valuation is primarily a Management Tool … but also a systematic analytical indication for financial purposes
>
> The primary objective is …
> - To provide a customised tool for the client to evaluate the strength of their brand portfolio
> - To provide a pragmatic framework for continuous usage
> - To provide a common language for discussions between different management levels and functions
> - To develop a proxy planning tool for making brand investment decisions"
>
> The Boston Consulting Group

More surprisingly, the accounting businesses also undertake brand valuations for strategic purposes, by understanding how brand strategy translates into value and share price, in addition to straightforward financial transactions.

> "Changing brand strategy – implications including internal and external management, change management and communication are integral to the success of improved brand and shareholder value."
>
> KPMG

What Is On Offer?

Despite the varying approaches that exist which we will review in this paper, they do fall into a number of categories and there are some consistencies in valuation techniques offered from the differing practitioners.

Whilst there are similarities in valuation approach, there are also undoubtedly great differences in the context in which brand valuation is offered from the range of practitioners.

Some practitioners are straight valuation experts; some are very flexible in the range of services they provide from an initial valuation through to detailed value-based strategy, and some use brand valuation as primarily a management tool within a specific strategic context.

Companies considering whether or not to undertake an assessment of brand value are well advised to seek independent guidance as to which type of approach would best suit their own individual situations, particularly when requiring comparable situations from differing practitioners.

For clarity and to avoid repetition, the technical approaches to brand valuation in the market have been grouped into the following categories, as reflected by the majority of practitioners.

- **Economic-based approach:** the value of the brand based on how much the business benefits from owning and using the brand.
- **Income approach:** the value of the brand based on the net value of earnings attributable to the brand. There are individual

financial methodologies based on the income approach, that are sometimes referred to individually as separate categories, such as **Royalty Relief and Premium Profits** (referred to as direct methodologies) and **Residual Earnings** (referred to as an indirect methodology).

Whilst different techniques, they are all based on the theme of identifying future earnings attributable to the brand over a particular period of time, and then discounting these back to present day values. This constituent element is common to both an Economic Use and an Income Approach, and has sometimes been referred to as an **Earnings Split**.

- **Market-based approach:** the value of the brand estimated using prices from market transactions involving the sale of comparable assets.
- **Cost-based approach:** the value of the brand based on the historical costs of creating the brand and the estimated costs of replacing or recreating the brand.
- **The asset-based or elimination approach:** the value of the brand based on subtracting the net tangible assets from the business' full market value.

It should be noted that some practitioners would use a particular technique (for example **Royalty Relief**) to identify the value of a brand for a number of differing situations – ranging from what it is worth in economic use to the business, as well as to form a market valuation.

As previously stated, the accounting and valuation practitioners tend to use a variety or combination of methodologies, depending on which is more appropriate to the individual situation, as well as to cross-check their findings and form an opinion of value.

They may also use some of their own valuation techniques such as **Real Options Valuation™** a probability analysis technique at PwC.

The management consultancies use a single model based on an income approach, and again may have developed their own valuation methodologies/techniques for certain situations.

For example at The Boston Consulting Group, **Brand Option Value®** identifies the future potential value of the brand based on strength and exploitation opportunities, and **Brand Flagship Value®** measures the attractiveness of a brand towards employees, other customers and potential investors.

A Deep Understanding Of The Consumer

Regardless of the technical methodology used to calculate the worth of a brand, in the majority of situations the one underlying and common approach to all, is the extensive and detailed qualitative and quantitative analysis of the brand internally and externally, prior to its assessment in financial terms.

The extent and structure of this research will depend on the nature of the valuation, the degree of information that exists already and the context in which the valuation is required, as well as the individual model used by the practitioner.

Usually this involves a comprehensive assessment and qualification of the brand through primary and secondary, internal and external research including:

- Financials and trading history (including margins and sales trends)
- The components of the brand within the value chain
- Detailed market segmentation
- History, heritage and longevity
- Competitive positioning and benchmarking
- Brand environment, positioning and profile
- Global reach
- Levels and effectiveness of marketing support for the brand

As well as looking to the future at:

- Trading potential
- Levels of market innovation
- Brand life cycles
- Levels of brand risk

The above is required in order to qualify (in particular with consumers), and quantify the market drivers, the brand value drivers and the brand equity.

Whilst the research obviously addresses the revenue generation of the brand, it also addresses the cost of support, which varies from business to business. For example BMW support its brand with substantial advertising, but its brand is also based on superior technology for which there is a cost. Similarly in retail there is a substantial property cost associated with flagship stores.

The research may often take a view on the strength of management, recognising the potential of 'fads', the lack of any true USP's in me-too brands, as well as shifts in consumer spending patterns.

The strength and quality of consumer data provides invaluable input to key valuation assumptions, including customer behaviour models. The real key in valuation is the interpretation of this information as a financial model.

All practitioners have their own individual ways of identifying, interpreting and assessing this information as a basis for their valuation methodology(s).

This may involve working with external specialist or research models that exist in-house.

The Individual Approaches
Economic Use Approach
This assesses the economic use of the brand based on what the brand is worth to the business.

For the purposes of clarifying this approach, an Economic-Use model is based on identifying the value of a brand as part of the intangible earnings returns of a business, specified as returns above the cost of capital.

> *"It seeks to value the asset as part of the ongoing business concern– i.e. its current use to its current owner, being a common reference"*
>
> *Brand Finance*

Economic-Use is a widely used term, but practitioners may use a variety of methodologies under this heading, which can cause confusion.

This model for calculating brand value is widely accepted by tax authorities worldwide.

It is based on identifying the incremental returns and earnings attributable to all intangible assets, through:

- Identifying the sales revenues from the brand
- Subtracting from this all the operating costs (including depreciation)

To identify:

- Earnings Before Interest, Tax and Amortisation
- And Net Operating Profit after Tax (NOPAT)
- Charges for capital employed are then subtracted from NOPAT
- Which then identifies intangible earnings overall

To then identify the specific earnings attributable to the brand, detailed research is undertaken to identify how the brand drives customer demand and what income and cash flow it generates for the business(s) in each individual market/customer segment.

Brand Strength analysis then identifies its strength and weaknesses and subsequent risk profiles in order to identify an appropriate brand discount rate.

Brand Value is calculated by taking a brand earnings forecast for a future period of time and using the brand discount rate to track it back to today's value.

The advantages to this methodology are that it focuses on future earnings or cash flow, facilitates comparisons and is widely accepted and understood. The disadvantages are a degree of subjectivity on cost allocation and assumptions and extensive information requirements.

Income-Based Approach

The value of a brand is estimated using the present value of earnings (profits) attributable to the brand asset.

Similar to an economic use approach but with greater emphasis placed on income i.e. earnings attributable to the brand with a cost for capital factored in, rather than earnings specified as returns above the cost of capital.

For the purposes of clarifying this approach, we have defined an income-based approach as one that identifies the value of a brand based on specifying the future forecast level of earnings that is attributable to the brand (after allowing for depreciation).

This is achieved by looking at past performance, as well as future performance on actual levels by:

- Identifying the net annual cash-flow from a business.
- Establishing which proportion of net margin is directly related to the brand (price premium or volume premium).
- Looking at the lifetime of a brand and determining future brand earnings and cash flows over a specific forecasting period.
- Identifying the right discount rate (in accordance to industry and incorporating a charge for capital), to apply to cash flow over this specific forecasting period.
- To use this discount rate to track back to the present time and to calculate the net present value of the brand.

As with an economic-use approach the aim is to identify the specific margin and earnings attributable to the brand. Detailed research is undertaken to identify how the brand drives customer demand and what income and cash flow it generates for the business(s) in each individual market/customer segment.

The income approach is very similar to the economic use approach, but with subtle differences such as how earnings attributable to intangibles are calculated and where costs for capital are factored in.

Sometimes an Income Approach to formulating brand value may use the following technical methodologies whose fundamentals remain broadly as above.

Direct Methods

Royalty Relief based approach: This provides the value of the brand based on a royalty from the revenue attributable to the brand being calculated.

The principle behind this method is identifying what royalty rate would need to be paid by a company for the use of a brand that it does not own.

This is by far the most commonly used single technique and methodology for calculating brand value. It is widely used to give an opinion of both market value and sometimes the economic use of a brand. In certain industries for example pharmaceuticals, hotels and garment manufacturing it is commonplace to license the use of the brand.

This methodology is again based on estimating the revenue attributable to the brand over its economic life.

Many practitioners have either their own, or access to, extensive databases of existing licensing agreements, whereby it is possible to identify the royalty rate paid for the use of comparable brands, which is usually expressed as a % of sales.

With existing brand revenue (sales) figures and an identified royalty rate, it is possible to calculate the difference between owning a brand rather than licensing it in.

This is calculated from identifying the future projected sales of a brand, estimating the royalty savings (after tax), and applying an appropriate discount rate back to present day value.

It has the advantage of being better for industries where the granting of licenses in exchange for a royalty payment is relatively simple and common, and is likely to be most appropriate for trademarks, patents and technologies. It is universally recognised by Revenue authorities worldwide.

It does, however, rely on some subjective information i.e. future forecasts of brand revenue allocations and the information being available on comparable royalty rates.

Premium Price (Profits)

Is conceptually very simple and based on identifying a 'base case comparison'.

For example, if a branded tin of baked beans retails for 50p and an unbranded tin of identical beans retails for 30p, then the annual premium profit is 20p, multiplied by the number of tins produced annually. The annual profit then needs to be capitalised, and a value based upon a view as to how long the brand maintains its market position, how the market will develop and the cost of keeping the brand up there.

This methodology is most useful for food and fmcg brands and relies upon being able to identify a generic product for base case comparison, which is not always possible.

The advantage of this procedure is that it is relatively simple to calculate. However, with the current retailing environment seeing increasing price pressures placed on manufacturers by the enormous buying power of the major multiples such as Tesco and Wal-Mart, profit margins are continually being eroded. This can have an adverse and inaccurate impact on the value of the brand.

The disadvantages are that it is very rarely that there are two direct comparables and that it maybe unfair to assume the entire price premium is due to the brand. Other factors such as quality of product and distribution may play a role.

Indirect methods

Maybe referred to as Residual Value or Residual Earnings Method, or Return on Assets.

This method is less robust than direct methods and can sometimes lead to anomalous results. It assumes normal returns for fixed assets and working capital of a business, and that brand value is the rest – the residual value.

It requires less assessment than other methods and therefore is less precise as to the contribution of the brand.

It is, however, widely used for US accounting purposes although more commonly used for non-brand intangibles with less readily identifiable cash flows.

It would not be a recommended approach individually, rather as a package of measures to crosscheck.

Market-Based Approach

A brand is valued by reference to prices of comparable assets in recent transactions, using multiples of revenue, gross margin, brand contribution and profit after tax, adjusted to reflect brands' differences.

If comparables exist, it is a relatively easy methodology and has the advantage of reflecting an actual similar market value. But it is rare that actual comparable transactions exist.

Overall, it may be an important indicator of value, but is mostly used as a crosscheck on other methodologies as sufficient information on recent transactions involving comparable brands is rarely disclosed.

"The principle advantage is that it is a practical approach which allows values to be based on real transactions and market evidence. This results in values that best reflect the price that would be negotiated between a third party buyer and seller.

The disadvantage is that there are relatively few third party arms' length transactions involving brand names that are directly comparable. There are more frequent transactions involving shares of companies owning brand names but it is usually difficult to allocate out value between business and brand name.

As a result historically, many values have tended to use income-based approaches as the principal valuation method.

The requirement of IFRS 3 to allocate value to material intangible assets including brands in a company acquisition, should improve the availability of market data on brand values."

KPMG

Cost-Based Approach

The value of the brand is calculated based on two cost options:

- Historical cost measuring the actual cost incurred in creating the brand.
- Replacement cost quantifying the estimated cost of replacing the brand or recreating an equivalent asset.

The advantages are that it is objective and can be consistent, if the information is readily available, which is not always the case. Historic cost data is reliable.

On the negative side, there is no correlation between expenditure on the asset and its value, it is also difficult to distinguish between brand maintenance and brand investment expenditure and replacement costs are subjective, particularly when looking at this approach in relation to entering a new market i.e. China. It may also not accurately reflect a fair market value for a brand.

It has limited range and appeal as a true measure of brand value, but can be a useful tool.

Asset-Based Approach Or Elimination Method

This approach values a business in its entirety as a market capitalisation, but then deducts the tangible assets to calculate the value of the intangible assets which will include patents, copyright, brands, customer lists, workforce, know how and goodwill.

Certain of these intangible assets can then be valued with reasonable levels of certainty; it is also possible to rank the most valuable to the least valuable of the identified intangible assets. It becomes possible to allocate the intangible asset value into each class and derive a value for the brand.

The advantages are that it is a simple and quick approach, which can then be used to benchmark the aggregate value of brands.

The disadvantages are that there is no guidance on how value should be allocated between a group of brand names. It also assumes that the market price is a fair price.

Again this is not a primary method due to its limitations, but can be a useful benchmark on the aggregate value of a company's brands.

What This Report Tells Us

> **There needs to be greater clarity in the definition of what constitutes a brand for valuation purposes**

Establishing common terminology in the market place for valuation purposes would significantly aid understanding and clarity in valuing brands.

> **There is no single 'correct' way to measure brand value**

Despite the obvious attractions and benefits of there being a single recommended approach to valuing brands, there is no 'one size fits all' that stands out head and shoulders above the rest.

Some approaches, for example Economic Use and Income-based which have some close similarities, are also more holistic than others. They are therefore much more useful in certain situations particularly for strategic purposes.

The use of a range of techniques to calculate the value of a brand is well established with some practitioners, who state that the circumstances drive the use of techniques and that relying on a single approach can throw up an anomalous result.

Greater clarity and consistency in the communication, description and relevance of approach from practitioners, would greatly assist in reducing confusion and drive forward a greater understanding in the marketing community.

Independent advice should always be sought on which direction is the best for the particular circumstances.

❯ Brand valuation ... more than another financial calculation it can be a strategic value enhancing model

A value credited to a brand is not just a black-box figure.

Despite the appearance of the methodologies as detailed financial calculations, the basis of identifying a qualified and quantified set of Brand Value Drivers and potential opportunities for growing Future Brand Value, is a fundamental for commercial success.

Detailed knowledge of the market, the company's position in that market in relation to competitors, and detailed consumer perceptions of a brand are all well established marketing principles. Qualifying and quantifying this information internally and externally within a model to derive a financial value on a brand, is a natural extension of performance management.

❯ Greater collective co-operation between finance and marketing

A value may already have been placed on a brand as an intangible asset on the balance sheet and the marketing department is either unaware of it or unaware of its potential relevance to brand and marketing strategies.

Relating brand and marketing strategy to value-growth and return on investment is the language of the Chief Executive and Finance Director, and will increase the strength of the relationship right across the Board.

Marketing people need to become more financially literate and equally, finance needs to become more marketing aware.

❯ The brand asset as security – use it

The value of the brand asset is increasingly being used as security in a wide range of situations, particularly in the private equity market.

This may include a company looking to raise finance for any number of reasons such as a management buy-out/buy-in or for future securitisation.

❯ Every business should conduct an overview of value in its brands

This might not necessarily involve a precise valuation, rather an understanding of what creates value in a brand or a portfolio of brands and how to make it work harder.

The value of the brand asset has often been over-looked in many businesses ranging from small to medium-sized companies, right through to larger conglomerates operating in less consumer-driven markets.

However, industrial and manufacturing companies across Europe are now waking-up to realising the value in their brands.

A recent article in the Financial Times 'Industry Plays The Name Game' (February 8th 2005) highlighted the extent that some engineering and industrial companies have gone to build the value of their brands, and the subsequent benefits this has brought.

> *"Having a good brand means you can compete in ways other than by having a lower price"*

> *FT February 8th 2005*

This same article also highlighted an example of what happened when not enough consideration was given to the value of brands:

> *"At Invensys, the UK engineering group established in 1998 after a merger of Siebe and BTR, pressure to integrate the businesses meant senior managers failed to devote enough attention to linking the different brands and divisions within the original companies.*

> *... A casualty of this was Foxboro, a well-regarded US-based maker of control equipment that had formerly been part of Siebe. It was discouraged from using its well-known brand name – one factor behind a subsequent slide in Foxboro's fortunes. Such setbacks exacerbated Invensys' problems and in 2001 the company suffered a series of financial disasters that brought it close to collapse."*

> *FT February 8th 2005*

Clearly understanding where the value lay in the portfolio of brands in this instance was a tool that could have aided both corporate restructuring and the creation of a new brand architecture.

❯ "The techniques used to value brands are merely a set of tools – the real skill is in the way the information is used to create growth and enhance value."

Jane Piper

A paper prepared by Jane Piper of Jane Piper Brand Strategy Consultancy on behalf of The Superbrands organisation

Brand Guardians

1Job.co.uk

JULIAN FELSTEAD
Managing Director and Brand Manager

Julian is the Managing Director and Brand Manager for 1Job.co.uk. For brand success he believes in three key principles: simplicity, honesty and that the brand image and company ethos reflects one another. Julian has a degree in Mechanical Engineering from Bath University.

KERRY TORCHIA
Technical Manager

Kerry is Technical Manager for 1Job.co.uk and is responsible for the design and look of the site. To him the brand represents a desire to provide a simple solution that enables job hunters to find all jobs in one place. Kerry has a degree in Computer Science from University of the West of England.

192.com

ALASTAIR CRAWFORD
Founder and CEO

Alastair Crawford launched 192.com in 2000. An internet entrepreneur, he was the first person to publish the Electoral Roll online, a UK directory enquiry site (192.com), and the first to challenge BT's monopoly of directory enquiries. Alastair, the inspiration and developer behind this award-winning website, has never been afraid to challenge monopolistic practices and his success in opening up the directory enquiries market has not only served 192.com well, but the directory industry as a whole. His aim now is for 192.com to become the obvious choice of search engine for finding people and businesses.

888.com

ITAI PAZNER
Global Offline Marketing Director

Itai joined 888.com in 2001. Coming from an ISP (Internet Gold) and drinks background his main focus as head of global offline marketing for the brand was the transition of Casino-on-Net into the now well known umbrella brand, 888.com. Other responsibilities include the development of the brand, overseeing all marketing communications and driving the company's future marketing direction.

MATT ROBINSON
Head of Offline Marketing UK

Matt joined 888.com in 2003 having held various senior marketing positions within the Pentland Group. Matt has been instrumental in establishing the brand as the market leader in the UK. He launched the brand in the UK market and is responsible for all marketing activities in the UK and Ireland including the implementation and development of the brand strategy and development.

allcures.com

MIKE RITSON
Managing Director & Superintendent Pharmacist

Mike is Managing Director and Superintendent Pharmacist for allcures.com and its high street stores. He has been integral in growing a large health information source and developments at allcures.com, which allow patients to access up to date information on medical conditions and treatments available from the online pharmacy.

PAUL SIMPSON
Marketing Director

Paul has been with allcures.com for over three years. His background in design, marketing and PR have helped allcures.com flourish online. Paul is head of the online side of Allcures group, expanding the company profile and keeping the website fresh and exciting for its ever increasing customer base.

Auto Trader

JONATHAN WILLIAMS
Head of Marketing, Trader Media Group

Jonathan joined Auto Trader in September 2001 as Head of Marketing, responsible for all marketing initiatives for autotrader.co.uk and biketrader.co.uk. Jonathan has over seven years experience in digital marketing across mobile, DTV and online. Since joining Auto Trader his role has expanded to cover Trader Media's complete digital portfolio as well as all trade marketing on both online and offline channels. Previously, Jonathan worked for Fish4 as Head of Strategic Alliances heading up online partners across Mobile, DTV and web. Previous to Fish4 Jonathan was based at YAC (Your always connected), specialising in unified messaging. As New Business Marketing Manager, Jonathan was responsible for a number of business elements, developing alliances with potential resellers as well as the internet marketing strategy.

bbc.co.uk

STEVE CONWAY
Head of Marketing, New Media

Steve joined the BBC in January 2000 as the Marketing Manager for BBC Radio Five Live. Prior to this he worked for KRAFT Foods and Groupe DANONE where he was International Marketing Manager. At the BBC his work has included the creation and implementation of new analogue, online and digital marketing strategies, the execution of new advertising campaigns – both on and off air – as well as the re-branding of Five Live and the BBC's New Media services. Steve took up his position of Head of Marketing, BBC New Media in 2001. He was responsible for the marketing launch of BBCi and the re-launch of bbc.co.uk in 2004. Currently he is working on the BBC's development of on demand services on the internet and digital television.

Boys Stuff

RICHARD NORTH
Founder

 From the early days of curry house conversations Richard has continued the original vision, to deliver both exceptional customer service and be first to market the latest gadgets. Richard believes the commitment to treating people as individuals and attracting others who share the same values, both as customers and work colleagues, has helped make Boys Stuff a market leader.

MAV PERI
IT & Operations Director

 Mav joined the Boys Stuff team shortly after the website's launch. Mav played a lead role in the creation of the ePandora operating system, a fully integrated and comprehensive front and back office system.

confetti

DAVID LETHBRIDGE
Chief Executive

 David is the Chief Executive and co-founder of confetti.co.uk. He was previously launch Marketing Director at LineOne (now owned by tiscali) and prior to that held senior consumer marketing positions with BT and Johnson & Johnson. David started his marketing career with Nestlé.

crocus

PETER CLAY
Marketing Director

 Before starting crocus, Peter was deputy Managing Director of BMP-DDB, the third largest advertising agency in the UK. He began as a graduate trainee and stayed for 16 years. Of all the clients he was involved in during that time, his longest association was with Volkswagen, an account he managed for 10 years. Peter is currently non-executive director of Bailey Robinson, the travel company.

MARK FANE
CEO

 Prior to crocus, Mark was the driving force behind Waterers Landscape, where he built it into the largest landscaping and contract maintenance company in the UK, with sales growing from £0.3 million to £24 million in 13 years. In 2003 he sold Waterers to ISS, the Danish facility services company. In 2000 Mark secured city backing to start crocus. He is presently a non-executive director of Ottakars plc, Graphite Capital and Royal Horticultural Society Enterprises.

Firebox

CHRISTIAN ROBINSON
Managing Director

 Since joining Firebox in 2000, Christian has held positions as Business Development Manager and Marketing Director, before taking up his current post of Managing Director in 2003. Firebox has become one of the most successful online retailers in the UK, having recently been featured in 13th place on The Sunday Times Virgin Atlantic Fast Track 100 list of the fastest growing privately owned companies in the UK.

MICHAEL SMITH
CEO

 Michael co-founded Firebox.com with university friend Tom Boardman in 1998 with the dream of retailing, marketing and manufacturing a select range of new and unusual products from around the world. Michael has recently launched a new company called Mind Candy Design, developing new genres of games and puzzles. The company launched with 'Perplex City' and is already a key player in the world of Alternative Reality Gaming.

Friends Reunited

MICHAEL MURPHY
Chief Executive

 Michael took over the helm at Friends Reunited in February 2003, following a successful management buy-in. Prior to joining the company he had a 20-year career with Pearson plc, including roles as Chief Operations Officer at FT.com and Managing Director of FT Business, culminating in being COO of the Financial Times Newspaper. He is also a Non-Exec Director of Datamonitor plc.

TIM WARD
Marketing Director

 Tim joined Friends Reunited in June 2003 from the Financial Times where he was Marketing Director for both the Newspaper and FT.com. Prior to this the majority of Tim's career had been spent in telecoms, including Bellsouth, Mercury one2one and from 1993 to 2000, Vodafone UK.

HalifaxHomeFinder

HomeFinder Team

 The HomeFinder team strives to ensure that the service provides excellent value for customers and meets their needs in finding the property of their dreams. One of the members of the business support team Mark Inch, has been in various roles within the estate agency industry since 1984. Mark undertook the core design of the product and continues to manage the innovation and strategic direction.

PAULA ROWNTREE
Marketing and Communications Manager

 Paula joined HBOS in 1988 and following a time managing the Marketing Team in Halifax Share Dealing, moved across to Halifax Estate Agencies in 2005. Here she is responsible for Marketing & Communication Strategy and Implementation. Having recently completed her CIM post-graduate Diploma in Marketing, she is looking forward to putting her experience into practice within the Estate Agency Industry.

JobServe

ROBBIE COWLING
Founder

 Robbie and his business partner John Witney formed JobServe in 1993. Prior to starting the company, both were IT contractors with no previous experience of running a business. Robbie has seen the company through many achievements and rapid growth to become one of the leading online recruitment advertisers in the UK. This success has been rewarded by a number of personal and company awards and inspired Robbie to guide the development of JobServe into new sectors and additional services for both advertisers and job-seekers alike.

Jobsite

KEITH POTTS
Managing Director, Jobsite UK (Worldwide) Ltd

 Keith is the Managing Director of Jobsite UK (Worldwide) Ltd, which he founded in September 1995 with his two brothers. Through Keith's vision and leadership Jobsite became one of the UK's fastest growing companies winning numerous awards. Jobsite was acquired by Associated New Media in 2004, allowing the team to succeed further in improving the Online Recruitment experience. Keith graduated from Brighton Polytechnic with a Computer Science and Statistics degree and has a background in software engineering. He lives with his young family in West Sussex.

Moonfruit

KEVIN FOSTER
Creative Lead

 Kevin has been the creative lead at Moonfruit for three years. Prior to this he worked as a graphic designer for 10 years for prestigious clients such as Disney, Sony, Cadbury, Nestlé and Endemol. Since joining Moonfruit, Kevin has been instrumental in designing both the Moonfruit brand and the user interface for its SiteMaker software.

JOE WHITE
Managing Director

 Joe is the Managing Director of Moonfruit, a role he has held for the past two years, having been Product Director prior to this. He is responsible for the overall SiteMaker product and brand, as well as the day to day running of the business. Previously to Moonfruit Joe was a consultant at McKinsey & Company.

MyTravel.com

RUSSELL GOULD
Director Of Digital Marketing

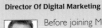 Before joining MyTravel to head up the group's digital marketing, Russell was Head of E-commerce at Bradford & Bingley, coming from the role of Product Development Director for the award-winning Charcolonline website. He had previously spent six years working in various product development, sales and marketing roles at ANZ Banking Group in New Zealand.

myvillage.com

ROIFIELD BROWN
Founder

 Prior to founding MyVillage, Roifield tried his hand at a number of business ventures including Audio Visual Design, Producer/Director and retail outlet owner. Originally named portowebbo, the brand's popularity increased dramatically when it changed to MyVillage in 2001. Roifield has been the leading force behind the brand's success. His business acumen and creative input continues to steer the company from strength to strength and he has seen the MyVillage brand grow to a dynamic network of 52 websites with over 600,000 users.

Nectar

RICHARD CAMPBELL
Marketing Director

 Richard joined LMUK as Marketing Director in January 2002, where he directed the launch of Nectar, which rapidly became the largest loyalty programme in the UK. Prior to LMUK, he held senior marketing positions at both Debenhams and the Burton Group. Before joining the Burton Group, Richard worked for a number of years in marketing services agencies and consultancies. Richard has a BA Honours degree in German from Durham University.

ROGER SNIEZEK
E-Commerce Director

 Roger joined LMUK in 2002 where he managed the launch of Nectar. He subsequently led the e-expansion of Nectar, culminating in the launch of Nectar eStores. Prior to LMUK Roger worked at Guinness and Forte Hotel Group in various IT, Project Management, and Marketing roles. Roger graduated from Cambridge University with a BA Honours degree in Mathematics.

NetNames

RODGER ARMSTRONG
Sales and Marketing Director

Rodger Armstrong is Sales and Marketing Director for Group NBT plc. Rodger is responsible for driving sales growth across the company and has day to day responsibility of the company's sales and marketing activities, including the NetNames Platinum Service business around the world.

GEOFF WICKS
CEO

Geoff Wicks came to Group NBT after a distinguished career at media giant, Reuters. Geoff has the overall responsibility of managing the company's brands, NetNames, NetBenefit and Easily.co.uk. Other responsibilities include developing the group's corporate strategy, to provide both management services for portfolios of domain names and hosting services.

PhotoBox

BEN FERRIER
Marketing Manager

Ben Ferrier joined PhotoBox in April 2002 and has helped build this fledgling brand up into the UK and Ireland's market leading online photo-sharing site. Ben's background in fine art and experience at eyestorm media has left him perfectly placed to help PhotoBox retain their market leadership whilst enabling him to implement creative campaigns to encourage growth.

GRAHAM HOBSON
CEO

Graham Hobson came up with the idea for PhotoBox in 1999, soon after the purchase of his first digital camera. Disappointed at the lack of UK-based photo-sharing websites, Graham gave up his career in the City and with friends created PhotoBox. Since its launch, the brand has gone on to become the UK and Ireland market leader. Graham remains very hands on with the brand, constantly looking for and implementing ways to grow the site and increase consumer satisfaction.

Times Online

PETER BALE
Online Editorial Director

Peter is a former editor for Reuters with assignments in Asia, the Middle East and Europe. He was a founder of the successful FTMarketWatch.com and has run his own web news consultancy with clients including MSN and Reuters.

SIMON CHRISTY
Marketing Manager

Simon joined News International in 2004 from Active ISP where he was the European Marketing Director. Simon is responsible for managing the Times Online brand, as well as increasing both site traffic and pay to view revenues.

toptable.co.uk

KAREN HANTON
Founder and CEO

Karen is the driving force behind toptable.co.uk and is widely known within the industry as a pioneer within new media. She has received significant public recognition including being named as one of today's top 30 entrepreneurs in New Business Magazine and voted one of the top 100 most influential people in the first decade of the internet in an NOP/e-consultancy poll.

CHRIS WOOD
Managing Director

Chris joined toptable.co.uk in January 2005 from Conran restaurants, where he was appointed Sales & Marketing Director in 2001. Chris is seen as an authority on the restaurant industry and is regularly asked to speak on both restaurant and marketing issues.

Totaljobs.com

SOPHIE RELF
Head of Marketing

When Sophie joined totaljobs.com she arrived with over six years publishing and media experience, five of which in the online recruitment industry. Having previous experience working in a business development role she enjoys a unique position of seeing recruitment from both sides, with a clear focus on matching employers with high calibre candidates. Sophie is a frequent speaker at HR events and lectures mature students at Business Schools. She is also a published author on career management and gives frequent career advice with contributions to national press and lifestyle magazines.

UpMyStreet

BARRY HOLLOWAY
Marketing Director

Barry Holloway formed part of the team that launched uSwitch in 2000 and helped acquire UpMyStreet in 2003. 'The uSwitch group is focused on helping people make smarter choices and UpMyStreet is an invaluable service in helping customers make important decisions about their home and local area'.

JANE RICH
Editor

Jane is responsible for adding news and feature content, increasing usage of the transaction tools, working with commercial partners and the overall editorial direction of the site. 'In this day and age communities need to be stronger than ever and I want to put UpMyStreet at the heart of that process.'

Glossary of Terms

ADSL – (Asymmetric Digital Subscriber Line). Refers to the method of transmitting data over traditional copper telephone lines at very high speeds.

Applet – A small software application, typically in the Java programming language.

Archive – A file that bundles together other files under a single name primarily for backup or transfer. It is often compressed to reduce the size or encrypted for privacy.

Attachment – A file included with an email or other form of message.

Avatar – A graphic facsimile that can be used in chat rooms.

Blog – See Weblog.

Bounced mail – Electronic mail that is returned undelivered to the sender.

Bps – (Bits per second). A basic measure of data transfer.

Broadband – High-speed internet access.

Browser – A software programme that enables you to view and interact with various kinds of internet resources available on the World Wide Web. Commonly referred to as a web browser.

CD-ROM – An acronym for Compact Disk Read-Only Memory, a storage medium for digital data.

Chat Room – An electronic space, typically a website or section of an online service, where people can go to communicate online in real time. Chat rooms are often organised around particular areas of interest, such as small business owners, gardening, etc.

Client – A programme that accesses information across a network, such as a web browser or newsreader.

Database – A structured format for organising and maintaining information that can be easily retrieved. A simple example of a database is a table or a spreadsheet.

DNS – (Domain Name System). The system that locates the numerical IP address corresponding to a host name.

Domain – The domain name is the unique name or address that identifies an internet site. Domain names always have two or more parts separated by dots. The domain name also identifies whether the site is part of a commercial (.com), government (.gov) or educational (.edu) entity.

Download – This is the method by which users copy software or other files to their computers from a remote computer.

Dotcom – A company that conducts its business on the internet.

E-mail – Short for electronic mail, sent from one user to another via a network.

E-mail address – The unique private internet address to which an e-mail is sent.

FAQ – (Frequently Asked Questions). A document that sets out to answer the most commonly asked questions on a specific topic.

File – Refers to anything stored on a computer, such as a programme, document or image.

FTP – (File Transfer Protocol). A common method for moving files across the internet.

Homepage – This is the starting point of a web presentation that acts as a sort of table of contents for what is at the website and offers direct links to other parts of the site.

Host – A computer that offers a variety of services to networked users.

HTML – (HyperText Markup Language). The language used to create web documents.

Hypertext links – The 'clickable' links or hotspots that interconnect pages on The Web.

Internet – An interconnected system of networks that connects computers around the world via the TCP/IP protocol.

IP address – This is a numeric code that uniquely identifies a particular computer on the internet. Just as a street address identifies the location of your home or office, every computer or network on the internet has a unique address too.

IPS – (Internet Service Provider). A company that provides and sells access to the internet.

Java – An object-oriented programming language developed by Sun Microsystems, to create self-running applications that can be easily distributed through the internet.

JPEG – A graphics file format widely used online because it combines good data compression (making images quicker to transfer) with good compatibility (all browsers can cope with them).

Junk email – See Spam.

Kbps – (Kilobits per second). The standard measure of data transfer speed.

LAN – (Local Area Network). A local network that connects computers spanning a relatively small area, such as an office or within the same building.

Link – This generally refers to any highlighted words or phrases in a hypertext document that enable a user to jump to a different section of the same document, or to another document on the World Wide Web.

Log on/Log in – To connect to a computer network.

Login name – This refers to the account name used to access a computer system. Also called user ID or user name it is the way people identify themselves to their online service or internet access provider.

Mailing list – A way to conduct a group discussion by electronic mail and distribute announcements to a large number of people simultaneously.

Mirror – A replica FTP or website set up to share traffic, when a website has become so popular that the volume of users accessing it is preventing others from getting through.

Modem – (Modulator/Demodulator). A device that enables remote computers to communicate with one another by using a standard telephone line.

Mouse menu – A custom menu that appears when you right click (by default) on screen items such as icons, web links and taskbars.

MP3 – A compressed music format.

Navigation tools – These allow users to find their way around a website or multimedia presentation. They can be hypertext links; clickable images; icons or image maps. They are normally found either at the bottom or top (or both) of each page or screen, and typically allow users to move around.

Network – Refers to two or more computers connected to each other to enable them to share resources.

Newsgroups – An electronic discussion group organised by subject hierarchies.

Offline – The state of being disconnected from a network, typically the internet.

Online – This can mean either the state of being connected to a network, typically the internet, or refer to a resource that is located on the internet.

Outlook – Microsoft's business e-mail programme that is incorporated into MS Office.

Ping – An echo-like trace that tests whether a host is available and what systems are working on the internet.

Plug-in – A programme that fits into another programme.

POP3 – (Post Office Protocol). An e-mail protocol that enables users to pick up mail from anywhere on the internet, even if they are connected via another users account.

Portal – A website that specialises in directing the user to other sites.

Protocol – The standard or set of rules that two computers use to communicate with each other.

Router – A piece of hardware or software that connects two or more computers or networks.

Search engine – A type of software that creates indices of databases, or internet sites, based on the titles of files, keywords or the full text of files. It has an interface that allows the users to type in a topic or word and then provides a list of search results.

Server – A computer that handles requests for data, e-mail, file transfers and other network services from other computers.

Spam – Junk e-mail and also the practice of blindly posting commercial messages or advertisements to a large number of unrelated and uninterested newsgroups.

Surf – Skip around the web from page to page by following links.

TCP/IP – (Transmission Control Protocol/Internet Protocol). The protocols that drive the internet.

Update – To bring a programme, version of a programme or data file up to date by installing a revision or a completely new version of it.

URL – (Uniform Resource Locator). The address for a resource or site (usually a directory or file) on the internet.

Usenet – A User's network, namely a collection of networks and computer systems that exchange messages and are usually organised by subject into newsgroups.

WAP – (Wireless Application Protocol). An agreed set of standards that determine how mobile phones and other devices connect to the internet.

The Web – (The World Wide Web or WWW). Graphic and text documents published on the internet that are interconnected through clickable 'hypertext' links.

Weblog – Commonly known as a blog. This is a journal-style personal webpage for which an individual or a group frequently generates text, photographs, video, audio file, and/or links, typically (but not always) on a daily basis.

Website – A collection of network services, primarily HTML documents, that are linked together and exist on The Web at a particular server.

Zip – A file compression format that is frequently used to reduce file size for transfer or storage on to floppy disks.

Index

Here you will find the nation's top web brands as voted by the eSuperbrands Council. Those featured in this publication are in bold.

BRAND	WEB ADDRESS	OTHER AREAS OF BUSINESS	BRAND	WEB ADDRESS	OTHER AREAS OF BUSINESS
DIY			**FINANCE**		
B&Q	www.diy.com	Home Improvements, Lifestyle	Bloomberg	www.bloomberg.co.uk	Resource, Stocks and Shares
			Cahoot	www.cahoot.co.uk	Mortgages, Personal Banking
			Egg	www.egg.com	Investment, Personal Banking
EDUCATION			Find	www.find.co.uk	Investment
Encarta	www.encarta.com	Encyclopaedia	Goldfish	www.goldfish.com	Insurance, Personal Finance
Open University	www.open.ac.uk	Resource	Intelligent Finance	www.if.com	Insurance, Personal Banking
			Interactive Investor		
			International	www.iii.co.uk	Investment, Resource
EMPLOYMENT			MoneyExpert	www.moneyexpert.com	Money Management,
1Job.co.uk	**www.1Job.co.uk**	**Recruitment**			Price Comparison
		(See page 16)	Money Extra	www.moneyextra.com	Resource
GoJobsite	www.gojobsite.net	Recruitment	Money Supermarket	www.moneysupermarket.com	Bargains and Best Deals,
jobsearch	www.jobsearch.com	Database, Recruitment			Money Management
JobServe	**www.jobserve.com**	**Database, Business**	**moneynet**	**www.moneynet.co.uk**	**Databases, Directories**
		(See page 58)			**(See page 66)**
Jobsite	**www.jobsite.co.uk**	**Database, Recruitment**	Moneywise	www.moneywise.co.uk	Money Management,
		(See page 60)			Price Comparison
Manpower	www.manpower.co.uk	Recruitment	Motley Fool	www.fool.co.uk	Money Management,
Monster	www.monster.co.uk	Database, Recruitment			Price Comparison
People Bank	www.peoplebank.com	Recruitment	One Account	www.oneaccount.com	Mortgages
Reed	www.reed.co.uk	Recruitment	PayPal	www.paypal.co.uk	Payment Transactions
Stepstone	www.stepstone.com	Recruitment	Smile	www.smile.co.uk	Internet Banking
Totaljobs.com	**www.totaljobs.com**	**Recruitment**	World Pay	www.worldpay.co.uk	Payment Transactions
		(See page 100)			
			FOOD AND DRINK		
			ASDA	www.asda.co.uk	Fashion, Retail
ENTERTAINMENT			Decanter	www.decanter.com	Wine Merchant
Faceparty	**www.faceparty.com**	**Social Networking**	Leaping Salmon	www.leapingsalmon.com	
		(See page 48)	ocado	www.ocado.co.uk	Retail
Firebox	**www.firebox.com**	**Gadgets and Gizmos**	Sainsbury's	www.sainsburys.co.uk	Home Delivery
		(See page 50)	Squaremeal	www.squaremeal.co.uk	Listings, Resource
			Tesco	www.tesco.com	Home Delivery, Retail
FASHION			**toptable.co.uk**	**www.toptable.co.uk**	**Listings, Resource (See page 98)**
Boden	www.boden.co.uk	Mail Order, Retail	Waitrose Food		
Figleaves	www.figleaves.com	Lingerie	Illustrated	www.waitrose.com/wfi	
La Redoute	www.redoute.co.uk	Mail Order, Retail			
Mango	www.mango.com	High Street, Retail			
Net-a-Porter	www.net-a-porter.co.uk	Designer, Trends	**GAMES**		
New Look	www.newlook.co.uk	High Street, Trends	Atari	www.atari.com	Downloads
River Island	**www.riverisland.com**	**High Street, Retail**	Electronic Arts Online	www.ea.com	Downloads
		(See page 84)	Nintendo	www.nintendo-europe.com	
Style.com	www.style.com	Trends	Shockwave	www.shockwave.com	Downloads, Retail
TOPSHOP	**www.Topshop.com**	**Retail, Trends (See page 96)**	Ubisoft	www.ubisoft.com	
FILM/THEATRE			**GARDENING AND FLOWERS**		
Internet Movie Database	www.imdb.com	Search Engines	**crocus**	**www.crocus.co.uk**	**Mail Order, Landscape Design**
Total Film	www.totalfilm.co.uk				**(See page 40)**

BRAND	WEB ADDRESS	OTHER AREAS OF BUSINESS	BRAND	WEB ADDRESS	OTHER AREAS OF BUSINESS
Flowers Direct	www.flowersdirectuk.co.uk	Gifts	**MOTORING**		
Greenfingers	www.greenfingers.com	Mail Order, Resource	AutoMart	www.automart.co.uk	Car Sales, Classifieds
Interflora	www.interflora.co.uk	Home Delivery	**Auto Trader**	**www.autotrader.co.uk**	**Car Sales, Classifieds**
					(See page 26)
			jamjarcars™	www.jamjar.com	Car Sales, Car Leasing
HEALTH			**What Car?**	**www.whatcar.com**	**Car Sales (See page 104)**
allcures.com	**www.allcures.com**	**Beauty, Remedies (See page 24)**			
eDietsUK	www.edietsuk.co.uk	Beauty	**MUSIC**		
ThinkNatural	www.thinknatural.com	Retail	CD WOW!	www.cdwow.co.uk	CD/DVD purchase
Net Doctor	www.netdoctor.co.uk	Pregnancy and Planning	HMV	www.hmv.co.uk	CD/DVD purchase
			iTunes	www.apple.com/uk/itunes	Downloads
			Ministry of Sound	www.ministryofsound.co.uk	Special Interest
INSURANCE			mp3.com	www.mp3.com	Downloads
Admiral	www.admiral.com		MTV	www.mtv.co.uk	Radio/TV sites
Churchill	www.churchill.com		mycokemusic.com	www.mycokemusic.com	Downloads
Confused.com	www.confused.com		Napster	www.napster.com	Downloads
Cornhill Direct	www.cornhilldirect.co.uk		Play.com	www.play.com	CD/DVD purchase, Games
Diamond	www.diamond.co.uk	Women's Sites	Real Music	www.realukmusic.co.uk	CD/DVD purchase
Direct Line	www.directline.com				
elephant.co.uk	www.elephant.co.uk				
Endsleigh	www.endsleigh.co.uk		**NAVIGATION**		
esure.com	www.esure.co.uk		Mapquest	www.mapquest.co.uk	Resource
marbles™	www.marbles.com	Travel, Personal Loans, Credit Card	Multimap.com	www.multimap.com	Resource
Mint	www.mint.co.uk	Credit Card, Personal Loans	**Streetmap**	**www.streetmap.co.uk**	**(See page 86)**
MORE THAN	www.morethan.com		**UpMyStreet**	**www.upmystreet.com**	**(See page 102)**
Pet Plan	www.petplan.co.uk	Pets	ViaMichelin	www.viamichelin.co.uk	
LEGAL			**NEWS AND MEDIA**		
OUT-LAW	**www.OUT-LAW.COM**	**Resource, Consultancy**	CNN	www.cnn.co.uk	Resource
		(See page 78)	**MAXIM**	**www.maximmag.co.uk**	**Celebrity, Fashion**
					(See page 64)
LIFESTYLE			NewsNow	www.NewsNow.co.uk	Business
50connect.co.uk	**www.50connect.co.uk**	**Communication,**	The Daily Mirror	www.mirror.co.uk	
		Social Networking (See page 20)	The Daily Telegraph	www.telgraph.co.uk	Business, Resource
confetti	www.confetti.co.uk	Gifts, Weddings (See page 38)	The Economist	www.economist.com	Business, Resource
Littlewoods			The Financial Times	www.ft.com	Business, Finance
even more	www.littlewoods.com	**Fashion, Gifts, Mail Order**	The Guardian	www.guardian.co.uk	Resource
		(See page 62)	The Independent	www.independent.co.uk	Resource
			The Onion	www.theonion.com	
			This Is London	www.thisislondon.co.uk	Listings
LISTINGS			**Times Online**	**www.timesonline.co.uk**	**Business, Resource**
myvillage.com	**www.MyVillage.com**	**Celebrity, Entertainment**			**(See page 92)**
		(See page 72)			
			PEOPLE FINDERS		
			Friends Reunited	**www.friendsreunited.co.uk**	**Social Networking**
LOYALTY SCHEMES					**(See page 52)**
Nectar	**www.nectar.com**	**Price Comparison, Shopping**	Genes Reunited	www.genesreunited.co.uk	Genealogy
		(See page 74)			

BRAND	WEB ADDRESS	OTHER AREAS OF BUSINESS	BRAND	WEB ADDRESS	OTHER AREAS OF BUSINESS
PHOTOGRAPHY			**TOURISM**		
digi-prints	www.digi-prints.com	Printing	**British Airways**		
PhotoBox	**www.photobox.co.uk**	**Printing (See page 80)**	**London Eye**	**www.ba-londoneye.com**	**Business Events, Leisure (See page 36)**
PROPERTY			**TRAVEL**		
Find A Property	www.findaproperty.co.uk		Bargain Holidays	www.bargainholidays.com	Flights, Holidays
Fish4	www.fish4.co.uk	Employment, Motoring	bmi	www.flybmi.com	Flights, Holidays, Resource
HalifaxHomeFinder	**www.halifaxhomefinder.co.uk**	**Estate Agents (See page 56)**	British Airways	www.ba.com	Flights, Holidays
Hot Property	www.hotproperty.co.uk		Cheapflights	www.cheapflights.com	Flights, Holidays
Primelocation.com	**www.primelocation.com**	**Database (See page 82)**	easyJet.com	www.easyjet.com	Bargains and Best Deals, Flights, Holidays
Property Finder	www.propertyfinder.co.uk	Database	ebookers.com	www.ebookers.com	Flights, Holidays, Price Comparisons
Rightmove.co.uk	www.rightmove.co.uk	Database	Expedia.co.uk	www.expedia.co.uk	Flights, Holidays
YOUR MOVE	www.your-move.co.uk	Database	First Choice	www.firstchoice.co.uk	Flights, Holidays
			Flybe	www.flybe.com	Bargains and Best Deals, Flights, Holidays
SHOPPING/PRICE COMPARISON			Hotels.com	www.hotels.com	Hotels
Argos	www.argos.co.uk	Mail Order	lastminute.com	www.lastminute.com	Bargains and Best Deals Flights, Holidays
Dixons	www.dixons.co.uk	Technology and Hardware	Latedeals.com	www.latedeals.com	Bargains and Best Deals Flights, Holidays
Dooyoo	www.dooyoo.co.uk	Technology and Hardware			
Froogle	www.froogle.google.co.uk		Lonely Planet	www.lonelyplanet.com	Guide Books, Resource
Letsbuyit	www.letsbuyit.com		**MyTravel.com**	**www.MyTravel.com**	**Flights, Holidays, Price Comparisons (See page 70)**
Next Directory	www.next.co.uk	Mail Order			
Price Checker	www.pricechecker.co.uk		National Rail Enquiries	www.railtrack.co.uk	Trains
Price Runner	www.pricerunner.co.uk		opodo	www.opodo.co.uk	Flights, Holidays, Price Comparisons
QVC.com	www.qvc.com		Priceline	www.priceline.com	Flights, Holidays, Price Comparisons
			Rough Guides	www.roughguides.co.uk	Equipment, Guide Books, Information
SPORT					
Football 365	www.football365.co.uk	News and Media	Ryanair	www.ryanair.co.uk	Flights, Holidays, Price Comparisons
Planet F1	www.planetf1.co.uk	News and Analysis	**teletextholidays.co.uk**	**www.teletextholidays.co.uk**	**Flights, Holidays Price Comparisons (See page 88)**
Planet Football	www.home.skysports.com	News and Media			
Planet Rugby	www.planetrugby.co.uk	Rugby	This Is Travel	www.thisistravel.co.uk	Flights, Holidays
Rivals	www.rivals.net		Travel Supermarket	www.travelsupermarket.com	Flights, Holidays
Sportal	www.sportal.com		Travelocity	www.travelocity.co.uk	Flights, Holidays
Sporting Index	www.sportingindex.com		Trip Advisor	www.tripadvisor.com	Equipment, Guide Books, Information
Sports.co.uk	www.sports.co.uk	News and Analysis, Search Engines	United Airlines	www.unitedairlines.co.uk	Flights, Holidays
TEAMtalk.com	www.teamtalk.com				
			TV AND RADIO		
TECHNOLOGY AND HARDWARE			Ananova	www.ananova.com/tv	Entertainment, News
Apple	www.apple.com	Downloads, Entertainment, Music	**bbc.co.uk**	**www.bbc.co.uk**	**Entertainment, News (See page 30)**
Dabs	www.dabs.com	Bargains and Best Deals	Discovery Channel	www.Discovery.com	Resource, Science and Nature
			Radio Times	www.radiotimes.com	Listings
TICKET CENTRES					
ticketmaster	www.ticketmaster.co.uk	Theatre/Film			

BRAND	WEB ADDRESS	OTHER AREAS OF BUSINESS	BRAND	WEB ADDRESS	OTHER AREAS OF BUSINESS
WEB			Silicon.com	www.silicon.com	Technology and Hardware
About.com	www.about.com	ISPs	supanet	www.supanet.com	ISPs
Acrobat Reader	www.acrobat.com	Software	**tiscali**	**www.tiscali.co.uk**	**ISPs (See page 94)**
Actinic	www.actinic.co.uk	Software	Tucows	www.tucows.com	Software
Adobe	www.adobe.com	Software	Virgin	www.virgin.net	ISPs
AltaVista	www.altavista.co.uk	Search Engines	Wanadoo	www.wanadoo.co.uk	ISPs
AOL	www.aol.co.uk	ISPs	Windows	www.windowsupdate.com	Software
Ask Jeeves	www.ask.co.uk	Search Engines	Yahoo!	www.yahoo.co.uk	Search Engines
Blogger	www.blogger.co.uk	Software	ZDNet UK	www.zdnet.co.uk	Technology and Hardware
Blue Yonder	www.blueyonder.co.uk	ISPs			
BT	www.bt.com	ISPs			
BTClickforBusiness	www.btclickforbusiness.co.uk	Technology and Hardware	**WEB HOSTING**		
Bulldog	www.bulldogbroadband.com	ISPs	easyInternetcafé	www.easyinternetcafe.com	Internet Café
Cisco Systems	www.cisco.co.uk	Technology and Hardware	Easyspace	www.easyspace.com	
Clara.net	www.clara.net	ISPs	Fasthosts	www.fasthosts.co.uk	
Cnet	www.cnet.co.uk	Technology and Hardware	NetBenefit	www.netbenefit.com	
Deckchair	www.deckchair.co.uk	Design			
Demon	www.demon.net.uk	ISPs			
Download	www.download.com	Software	**WOMEN'S SITES**		
easynet	www.easynet.co.uk	ISPs	Handbag	www.handbag.com	Celebrity, Fashion
Epson	www.epson.co.uk	Technology and Hardware	iVillage	www.ivillage.co.uk	
Excite	www.excite.com	Search Engines			
Google™	**www.google.co.uk**	**News and Analysis, Search Engines (See page 54)**	**YOUTH**		
			dubit	**www.dubit.co.uk**	**Social Networking (See page 44)**
HP	www.hp.com	Technology and Hardware			
Intel	www.intel.co.uk	Technology and Hardware			
Java	www.java.sun.com	Software			
looksmart	www.looksmart.com	Browsers			
Lucent	www.lucent.co.uk	Technology and Hardware			
LYCOS	www.lycos.co.uk	ISPs			
McAfee	www.macafee.co.uk	Domain Names			
Macromedia Flash Player	www.macromedia.com	Software			
Microsoft Hotmail (MSN)	www.hotmail.com	E-mail Services			
Microsoft Outlook	www.microsoft.com/outlook	E-mail programmes			
Moonfruit	**www.moonfruit.com**	**Hosting, Software (See page 68)**			
Moreover	www.moreover.com	News and Analysis Technology and Hardware			
Mozilla	www.mozilla.org	Software			
Netscape	www.netscape.co.uk	Browsers			
NetNames	**www.netnames.com**	**Domain Names (See page 76)**			
Nominet	www.nominet.co.uk	Domain Names			
NTL	www.ntl.com	ISPs			
One.Tel	www.One.tel.co.uk	ISPs			
Oracle	www.oracle.co.uk	Technology and Hardware			
PC World	www.pcworld.co.uk	Retail, Technology and Hardware			
Pipex	www.pipex.net	ISPs			
Real Player	www.real.com	Software			
Safari	www.apple.com/safari	Browsers			
Scoot	www.scoot.co.uk	Search Engines			

Directory

1Job.co.uk
Direct Recruit Ltd
74 High Street
Sutton Benger
Chippenham
SN15 4RL

192.com
i-CD Publishing (UK) Ltd
Units 8-10
Quayside Lodge
William Morris Way
London
SW6 2UZ

50connect.co.uk
10MEDIA.NET plc
5 Church Street
Windsor
Berkshire
SL4 1PE

888.com
888 Holdings plc
607-701
Europort
Gibraltar

allcures.com
Allcures plc
Allcures House
Arisdale Avenue
South Ockendon
Essex
RM15 5TT

Auto Trader
Auto Trader
41-47 Hartfield Road
Wimbledon
London
SW19 3RQ

Avon
Avon Cosmetics Ltd
Nunn Mills Road
Northampton
NN1 5PA

bbc.co.uk
BBC New Media
BC5 C4 The Broadcast Centre
202 Wood Lane
London
W12 7TP

Betfair
Betfair
Waterfront
Hammersmith Embankment
Chancellor Road
London
W6 9HP

Boys Stuff
BOYS STUFF Ltd
Vulcan House, Vulcan Road
Oxford Industrial Park
Bilston
West Midlands
WV14 7LF

British Airways London Eye
British Airways London Eye
Riverside Building
Westminster Bridge Road
London
SE1 7PB

confetti
Confetti Network
80-81 Tottenham Court Road
London
W1T 4TE

crocus
crocus.co.uk Ltd
Nursery Court
London Road
Windlesham
GU20 6LQ

DatingDirect.com
DatingDirect.com Ltd
The Axis
Holliday Street
Birmingham
B1 1TF

dubit
Dubit Ltd
2 Moorfield Chambers
Moorfield Crescent
Leeds
LS19 7EA

eBay.co.uk
eBay UK
PO Box 659
Richmond Upon Thames
Middlesex
TW9 1TX

Faceparty
CIS Internet Ltd
Great Bardfield
Essex
CM7 4SL

Firebox
Firebox.com Ltd
Firebox House
Ardwell Road
London
SW2 4RT

Friends Reunited
Friends Reunited
2 Oxted Chambers
185-187 Station Road East
Oxted
Surrey
RH8 0QE

Google™
Google
Belgrave House
76 Buckingham Palace Road
London
SW1W 9TQ

HalifaxHomeFinder
Halifax Estate Agencies Ltd
Trinity Road
Halifax
HX1 2RG

JobServe
JobServe Ltd
Tower Business Park
Tiptree
Essex
CO5 0LX

Jobsite
Jobsite UK (Worldwide) Ltd
Langstone Technology Park
Havant
Hampshire
PO9 1SA

Littlewoods even more
Littlewoods Shop Direct Group
Skyways House
Estuary Commerce Park
Speke Road
Speke
Liverpool
L70 1AB

MAXIM
Dennis Publishing
30 Cleveland Street
London
W1T 4JD

moneynet
Moneynet
2nd Floor
Sussex House
8-10 Homesdale Road
Bromley
BR2 9LZ

Moonfruit
Greek Attic Ltd
50 Greek Street
London
W1D 4EQ

MyTravel.com
MyTravel UK Ltd
Holiday House
Sandbrook Way
Rochdale
OL11 1SA

myvillage.com
MyVillage
105 Ladbroke Grove
London
W11 1PG

Nectar
Loyalty Management UK Ltd
3rd Floor
80 Strand
London
WC2R 0NN

NetNames
Group NBT plc
Prospero House
241 Borough High Street
London
SE1 1GA

OUT-LAW
Pinsent Masons
30 Aylesbury Street
London
EC1R 0ER

PhotoBox
PhotoBox Ltd
2-3 Park Royal Metro Centre
London
NW10 7PA

Primelocation.com
Bespoke Communications
12 Harley Street
London
W1G 9PG

River Island
River Island Clothing Co. Ltd
Chelsea House
Westgate
London
W5 1DR

Streetmap
Btex Ltd
PO Box 5123
Milton Keynes
MK5 6WY

teletextholidays.co.uk
Teletext Holidays
Building 10
Chiswick Park
566 Chiswick High Road
London
W4 5TS

ThomsonLocal.com
Thomson Directories
296 Farnborough Road
Farnborough
Hampshire
GU14 7NU

Times Online
TNL Newspapers Ltd
Times Online
1 Pennington Street
London
E98 1NN

tiscali
Tiscali UK
20 Broadwick Street
London
W1F 8HT

TOPSHOP
Topshop
Colegrave House
70 Berners Street
London
W1T 3NL

toptable.co.uk
toptable.co.uk Ltd
33 Welbeck Street
London
W1G 8EX

Totaljobs.com
Totaljobs.com
Holden House
57 Rathbone Place
London
W1T 1JU

UpMyStreet
UpMyStreet
Portland House
Stag Place
London
SW1E 5BH

What Car?
Haymarket Publishing Ltd
60 Waldegrave Road
Teddington
Middlesex
TW11 8LG

Yell.com
Yell
Queens Walks
Oxford Road
Reading
RG1 7PT